THE
PREGNANCY
EXERCISE BOOK

THE
PREGNANCY
EXERCISE BOOK

BARBARA DALE & JOHANNA ROEBER

Foreword by Irwin H. Kaiser, M.D., Ph.D.

PHOTOGRAPHS BY SANDRA LOUSADA

PANTHEON BOOKS, NEW YORK

To my children and friends who have
encouraged me and to one special friend who
always found time to listen.
Johanna Roeber

To Michel Odent, Elizabeth Kubler-Ross and the
other prophets who take us on to the New Age
at birth, throughout life and through death.
Barbara Dale

Foreword copyright © 1982 by Irwin H. Kaiser, M.D.
Text copyright © 1982 by Barbara Dale
and Johanna Roeber
Photographs copyright © 1982 by Sandra Lousada

Conceived, edited and designed by
Frances Lincoln Ltd,
91 Clapham High Street, London SW4 7TA, England.

Originally published in Great Britain as
Exercises for Childbirth
by Century Publishing Co. Ltd, London.

Library of Congress Cataloging in Publication Data
Dale, Barbara.
  The pregnancy exercise book.

  Bibliography:p.
  Includes index.
    1. Pregnancy. 2. Exercise for women. 3. Pre-
natal care. 4. Postnatal care. I. Roeber,
Johanna. II. Title.
RG558.7.D34   618.2'4   82-47876
ISBN 0-394-52730-5   AACR2
ISBN 0-394-71119-X (pbk.)

Manufactured in Italy
First American Edition

Contents

Williams' Obstetrics, the first modern American textbook on the subject of pregnancy and birth, was published almost 80 years ago; it prescribed for pregnancy "as much outdoor exercise as possible," consisting of "walking or driving, but the ordinary sports should be interdicted."

Eastman's Expectant Motherhood, published in 1940 and for a generation the most widely read popular book of advice to pregnant women, advised walking, gardening and light housework. Horseback riding, tennis and skating were discouraged, but golf was permissible and dancing was considered harmless if indulged in moderately.

The Pregnancy Exercise Book, which you are about to read, represents an entirely different point of view – the view that childbirth itself is athletic and often balletic, and that preparation helps. It is truly liberated from the Victorian epoch in obstetrics, which began when Queen Victoria chose a chloroform anesthetic for the birth of her seventh child.

The beginning of the end of that epoch came in 1944, when Grantly Dick Read argued in *Childbirth Without Fear* that pain resulting from tension was the enemy of natural childbirth. His prescriptions for education and exercises reestablished the pregnant and laboring woman in a vigorous central role, and thus set the stage for what has followed.

The Pregnancy Exercise Book is the product of many concepts that have emerged and gained acceptance in recent years. One is the recognition that health-care consumers generally benefit when they are as well informed as possible. That women should learn as much as they can about pregnancy and labor seems obvious. That they should also question doctors and midwives and hospitals on the basis of that knowledge has disturbed many health professionals. The authors of this book have sensibly made suggestions for such inquiries, the goal of which is constructive.

Barbara Dale and Johanna Roeber's basic premise is that one of the best ways for pregnant women to participate in their own care is by assuming an active role in a program of physical exercise. They recognize that no one exercise or group of exercises will suit everyone. But a well-balanced program, such as the one offered here, will not only enhance pregnancy but also help prepare women to take an active role in a normal process – their own labor.

Such an approach seeks to minimize artificial intervention. Both fetal monitoring by electronic recorders and fetal blood sampling do in fact intrude on normal processes. It seems wise to employ them only when pregnancy and labor may have deviated from a healthy course. Such technology has unquestionably saved the lives of some babies and protected many others from subtle injury with possible lifelong effects, especially on the central nervous system. Unfortunately, these technologies are often routinely employed in what the authors call a "sterile, impersonal environment." In hospitals where the surroundings for childbirth are warm, supportive and clean, and where the need for monitoring is explained if such a need arises, birth technology falls into its proper place. With such places available, and with women increasingly inclined to take responsibility for the kind of treatment they receive, there is no need to retreat to the risks of home birth in order to have a satisfying childbirth experience.

The belief that women should be able to control what happens to their bodies and their lives is the vital center of the women's movement. In pregnancy and labor this control takes an intriguing form – it involves letting go. It is essential at the end of pregnancy that labor be a form of release, resulting in the baby's own release from the mother's body. If women are educated to trust their bodies, to be sensitive to what their educated instincts tell them, they may thereby achieve control of the release of normal labor.

The Pregnancy Exercise Book makes repeated reference to the role of the woman's partner during pregnancy and labor. It was observed long ago that the most common fear of laboring women is the fear of being left alone. Indeed, the derivation of the word midwife is that of someone "with the woman." It has now been recognized that the partner can and should be brought into the labor room and that this is appropriate even in the most technological of environments. And the partner need no more be a man than the doctor or midwife need be a woman.

In summary, *The Pregnancy Exercise Book* is in rhythm with the best contemporary ideas about pregnancy and childbirth. Those of us who have watched the changes in obstetrics of the last four decades with awe, astonishment and an awareness of accomplishment will acknowledge this book as a worthy and highly readable addition to our arsenal of educational tools.

IRWIN H. KAISER, M.D., Ph.D.
Professor of Gynecology and Obstetrics
Albert Einstein College of Medicine, New York

Today, when women become pregnant, they look forward to a birth that is not only safe but also satisfying. Thanks to modern obstetrics, doctors and midwives can be relied on to act effectively in cases of emergency. As most women have a normal pregnancy and an uncomplicated labor, the fear is no longer of death at childbirth but rather of disappointment at the quality of the experience. Most women can't recall how they felt at their own birth, but they know that the experience of giving birth will remain vibrant and dramatic for the rest of their lives. They want to prepare themselves for the kind of birth they seek, to take responsibility for their pregnancies and so give their families the best possible start. This book is designed to bring out the instinctive knowledge and strength that every woman has within her.

We recognize that women want to feel confident in their bodies as they progress through pregnancy to childbirth. They want to keep fit and well during these months of waiting. They want to make positive preparation for the birth itself, so that they can go into labor confident that they can guide their bodies, in their own way, through the pain of contractions. And after the birth, they want to get back to normal physical activity as soon as possible.

All the exercises in this book are safe and gentle: while they stretch and strengthen your muscles, they don't require much more exertion than most

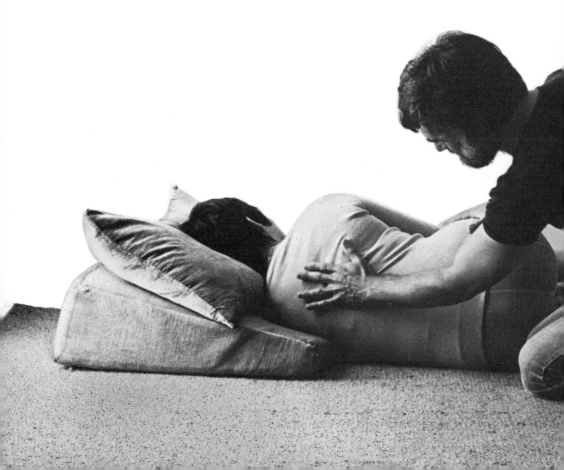

everyday activities. The aim should be to exercise little and often: respect the messages that your body gives you, rest when you're tired and if you feel any sudden or sharp pain, stop whatever you're doing. If you're going to dance or exercise classes, it's essential to mention to your teacher that you're pregnant as soon as possible. During a normal pregnancy, the movements suggested in this book can do you no harm, but if you're at all worried, consult your doctor before you start. It's particularly important to take your doctor's advice if there are any complications or if you have been warned that there's a possibility of a miscarriage.

This book presents a range of resources for every woman to draw on – posture and movement, relaxation, breathing and massage. It does not lay down a rigid discipline, but rather sets forth basic, easy-to-learn skills, many of which involve the partner or friend who will support you during labor. It encourages you and your partner to adapt those that work best for you and to use them not only during pregnancy and labor but for the rest of your lives. The practical techniques learned from this book, and the confidence in your body and yourself that they will give you, will enable you to feel your best during pregnancy, to cope with the stresses of labor and to make childbirth a joyful experience for you, your partner and your baby.

Before becoming pregnant for the first time many women are surprisingly unaware of the internal workings of their own bodies. However, once the pregnancy is confirmed, the pelvis and its associated muscles and organs become the center of interest. It's important to understand the role of the pelvis in pregnancy and childbirth, both for your sake and for the sake of the baby.

Getting to know yourself

The pelvis
The bones of the pelvis form the strong frame that acts like a cradle, surrounding, supporting and protecting the womb. To get to know your pelvis, begin by putting your hands on your hips – you'll feel the upper, outer edges. With one hand follow the edge of the bone down the front of your body, noticing the curve. Continue until you feel the hard ridge of your pubic bone and keep your hand there. With your other hand follow the edge of your pelvis back until you feel where your spine and your pelvis meet; then run your hand down your spine until it disappears between your buttocks. The space between your hands, the lower opening of the pelvis, is filled with layers of muscle called the pelvic floor. During labor, your baby descends through the lower opening of your pelvis, stretching the muscles of the pelvic floor to widen the vagina.

The pelvic floor
This is the essential sling of muscle that helps to hold the pelvic organs in place. Several layers deep, the pelvic muscles are slung under the pelvis in two intersecting circles, which look like a figure eight. The larger, top ring of muscle controls the outlets of the urethral and vaginal sphincters; below is the smaller circle of muscle, which contains the stronger anal, or rectal, sphincter. The muscles overlap and so they are thicker at the perineum, the area between the anus and vagina (see opposite).

Self-examination
If you have never looked at yourself, now is the time to start. Pelvic examinations are an almost inevitable part of pregnancy and labor, and this official inspection makes some women, and sometimes their partners, feel that the

The bones of the pelvis

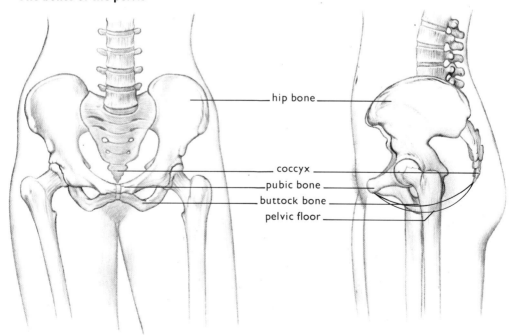

hip bone

coccyx
pubic bone
buttock bone
pelvic floor

most personal and private part of their bodies has become public property. This can deeply affect how a woman feels about her sexuality and can lead to her feeling that sex-play, making love and pregnancy somehow don't go together. Exploring the area yourself, or with the help of your partner, makes it seem less secret and mysterious.

Look at the diagram below and try to visualize your own body. Remember that everyone is slightly different and that no one is completely symmetrical. Either squat naked over a mirror or lie down and prop one up so you can have a closer look at yourself. Look at the relationship of the three outlets to each other and feel how the sensitivity to touch varies considerably in such a compact area. Gently introduce a clean finger into your vagina, noticing how stretchy and soft it is when relaxed; feel the difference when you tighten your muscles. Look again at the

diagram and try to visualize your pelvic floor.

Think of a small grapefruit – your baby's head will be about the same size as it journeys down the birth canal. Look at the illustrations of positions for labor on pages 98–105: try one out and imagine that you are letting your pelvic floor muscles relax and open up at the beginning of the second stage of your labor. It's the same sensation of opening up and giving that you feel when you naturally relax your pelvic floor to allow your partner's penis to enter your body during love-making.

It may seem impossible that your body could accommodate the stretch as your baby's head passes through your pelvic floor, and that it could do so with relative ease, but it will. The muscles of the vagina are like a kilt – when the pleats are ironed out flat the kilt is much bigger than when it's pleated up. In the same way, your vagina will be able to stretch round your baby's head and body during delivery.

The pelvic organs and the pelvic floor

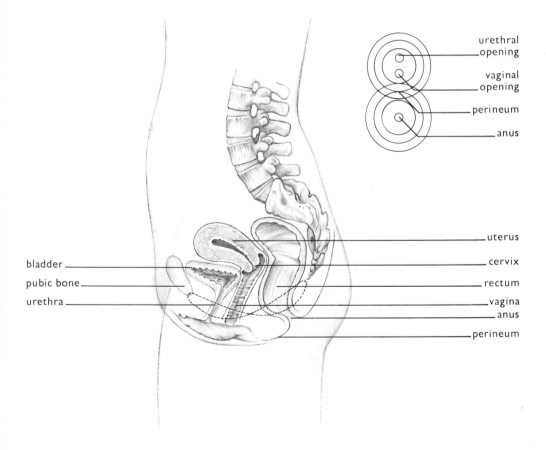

Caring for the pelvic floor

Pelvic floor exercises are important throughout your life. Sensitivity in this area increases your enjoyment of love-making: if the muscles become slack over the years, you'll find that you don't enjoy sexual intercourse as much and may have difficulty reaching orgasm; your partner will also find love-making less enjoyable. Eventually, a weak pelvic floor can lead to incontinence and even prolapse – sagging of the walls of the vagina – whereas a healthy pelvic floor gives the confidence of feeling in control. It's especially important to do pelvic floor exercises during pregnancy, because there is a natural increase of the hormone progesterone, which softens fibrous tissues and ligaments and allows the joints of the body to stretch more easily. This process also softens the pelvic floor and, as the baby grows, the extra weight pressing down may weaken it. Strengthening the muscles helps prevent problems such as incontinence when you laugh or sneeze, or a general dragging feeling when you stand or walk.

In the second stage of labor, active awareness of the pelvic floor muscles helps you to cooperate with the midwife and so lessens the risk of a tear. After the birth, exercising these muscles helps the vagina to return to its original pre-pregnant condition quickly. A healthy pelvic floor may also heal faster if you do tear or have to have stitches.

Testing your sensitivity

The enjoyable way to test the strength and sensitivity of your pelvic floor is during love-making. When your partner's penis is inside your vagina, squeeze and release your pelvic floor several times. He can tell you immediately how effectively your muscles are working. If you think you're squeezing hard and he reports not feeling much, then you'll know that your pelvic floor needs strengthening. Another way to test your control is to try to stop the flow when you urinate. If you can cut it off completely, and can re-start and then stop again, your muscles are in good shape. Do make sure that you empty your bladder completely after trying this exercise.

The drawbridge exercise

This is the essential pelvic floor exercise. It's best learned lying down, so you're not pulling up against gravity. Lie on your back with your knees bent up, hip-width apart, and your feet flat on the floor. Make yourself comfortable, with a cushion under your head. Flatten your shoulders and let your hands and arms relax.

Your aim is to tighten the pelvic floor muscles in four or five progressive stages, pausing slightly after each squeeze, and then to do the same in reverse, as you let go. Tighten the muscles a little and then stop – imagine you are lifting a drawbridge inside you. Close your eyes, trying to focus on the movement inside your body. Repeat, tightening a little more each time, until you can pull up the drawbridge no farther. Hold this squeeze while you slowly breathe in and out a couple of times. Make sure your face and lower jaw are quite relaxed. Let the drawbridge down in as many stages as you can manage and not just in one big crash: let go a little, pause for a moment, then release again and so on. Always finish the exercise with a tightening squeeze and lift – you don't walk about with your mouth hanging open, so don't forget your pelvic floor either.

When you've mastered this exercise lying down, try it sitting, standing and walking. There is no need to hold it for long; it's better to repeat it often.

Practice it every time you:
- Brush your teeth
- Go up and down stairs
- Answer the telephone
- Stop at the traffic lights
- Feel tired or depressed.

As you exercise your pelvic floor, you may realize that you are unconsciously tightening your thighs or pursing your mouth. During labor, it's helpful to be able to allow one group of muscles to work without tensing others, so start practicing this muscular isolation now. For example, try tightening your pelvic floor; hold it while you contract your thigh muscles. Allow your pelvic floor to relax while your thighs remain tight and finally relax your thighs. Make sure you keep your breathing gentle and regular. Finish by giving your pelvic floor a tightening squeeze.

Practice for delivery

Having built up your awareness and control you can start practicing for the second stage of labor. Learn how easy it is to allow your pelvic floor to open up. This helps your baby descend through your body: you give birth by letting your pelvic floor give.

Squat down and tighten your pelvic floor muscles as much as you can. Now take a slow breath in. As you sigh your breath out, allow the muscles to relax in one continuous letting-down movement. It's important to relax your mouth as your baby is coming out, as there's a sympathetic relationship between your mouth and your vagina, so always keep your mouth soft, smiling and open when you practice for labor. Make sure your partner is aware of this and can help you on the birth day.

If you don't feel your pelvic floor bulging open, make a fist with one hand over your mouth and blow firmly into it: you should feel a much stronger opening-up sensation. When you've finished the exercise, give your pelvic floor a quick lift and squeeze.

Practice this exercise while you squat and in other birth positions (see pages 98–105), so you become familiar with opening your pelvic floor in any position that you might want to use. If you try it lying on your back, you'll find that your vagina seems to be less responsive and that you have to work much harder to feel the muscles open up – this is one of the reasons why squatting is a good position for delivery (see pages 102–3 for other reasons).

Exercises for the pelvis

The following movements will help you prepare the pelvic area for childbirth. Practice them in rhythmic slow motion, repeating each movement about six times; you don't need to set aside time for them – they're easy to work into your daily routine. By learning to move your pelvis with greater ease and confidence, you can find the best position for yourself and your baby during labor.

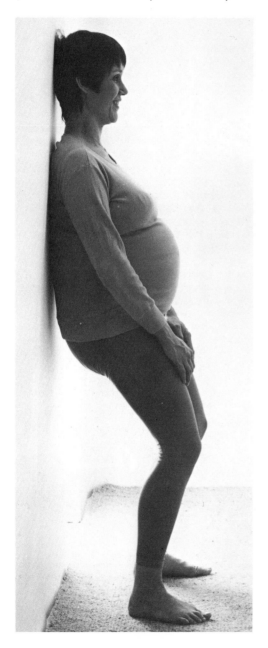
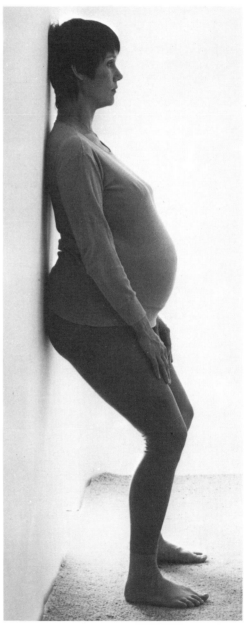

far left The pelvic tilt is an essential movement for maintaining good posture during pregnancy and after the birth (see also pages 19–24). For when you tilt your pelvis, by lifting the pubic bone up in front, the abdominal and buttock muscles are most effectively able to support the trunk, and strain on your lower back is minimized.

To learn the movement, stand with your feet a little way from a wall, hip-width apart. Bend your knees slightly and rest your back, shoulders and head against the wall. Breathe in. As you breathe out, press your lower back firmly against the wall, pulling in your abdomen and lifting your pubic bone, so your buttocks tighten and leave the wall. Keep your shoulders on the wall, so you learn to move the pelvis only.

Once you've mastered the tilt, you can do it in any position – kneeling, sitting, bending forward or on all fours. You can also practice it lying on your back or on your side, perhaps in the bath; or you can try it in any of the labor positions. It needn't be an exaggerated movement – just do a few small tilts every day. When you're confident, combine them with the drawbridge exercise on page 13, and make the two together a habit for the rest of your life.

above Kneel with your knees in line with your hips and your hands in line with your shoulders (left). Make sure your back is as flat as if you were balancing a tray of glasses on it. At first, it helps to have a partner to check you're not letting your lower back sag. Pull in your abdominal muscles, tighten your buttocks and do a pelvic tilt, so your back humps up (right). Don't rock your pubic bone back in this position, or when leaning forward, as the extra weight you're carrying and the pull of gravity might strain your back.

above Find a table or surface that comes up to about your hip level. Standing with your feet hip-width apart, lean forward with a straight back and rest your hands on the surface. Do a pelvic tilt, so your back humps up in the same way as before.

left Do a pelvic tilt and then reverse the action by dropping your pubic bone down and back. Try it first against a wall to check that you're moving your pelvis only, and not your shoulders. Rock your pelvis back and forth, finishing with a pelvic tilt.

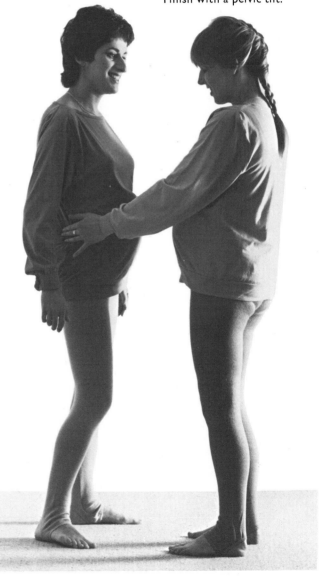

below Stand with legs slightly bent and put your hands firmly on your hips to help you move your hips only, rather than allowing your whole body to sway; you can do this with a partner, too. Slowly make a large circle with your coccyx, emphasizing the forward movement. Repeat the opposite way. Finish with a pelvic tilt.

above Stand with your legs a little apart. Keeping them straight, lift one and then the other, walking in place. If you rest your hands on your hips, you will feel your pelvis rock from side to side. Once you're used to doing the lifting movement with straight legs, bend your knees and try it with both legs bent.

Dancing is an excellent way of combining business with pleasure. Rocking and circling the pelvis are basic movements in all rhythmic dance. Try pelvic dancing to music – standing, kneeling or on all fours. This is a comforting movement during labor, whatever position you're in.

left Twisting with a towel as you dry your lower back after a bath or shower is an easy way of practicing pelvic movement. Stand with your knees slightly bent, holding your towel round your lower back. As you pull the towel from side to side, gently twist your pelvis: one hip coming forward with each hand, as if you were dancing. Start slowly and if it feels comfortable, speed up.

below Kneel on all fours, with a cushion under your knees, if necessary. Move your pelvis slowly from side to side, as if you were a large lazy dog wagging a very heavy tail. Look round at each hip as you bring it forward. Remember to keep your back horizontal.

When you're pregnant, it's important to be aware of the effect your changing weight is having on your posture and to adjust it accordingly to maintain a state of harmonious balance. The rocking movements and small adjustments below are aimed at helping you find your center of balance, from the early months of pregnancy until the last few weeks. First try these movements standing in front of a mirror; when you're used to the feeling of standing well, apply the same principles of balance and ease as you move about, sit or lie – good posture should be dynamic, alive and always changing according to your needs.

How to achieve good posture

- Stand with your feet hip-width apart, so that your legs fall straight down from the hip joints.
- Have your feet in line with one another, turning outward no more than a fraction.
- Rock back and forth between the heels and the balls of your feet to find the central point at which your weight is well balanced over the whole of each foot. Make sure the arches remain lifted, so you're not rolling your feet either inward or outward.
- Bend your knees very slightly, so they are at ease and are not braced tightly back.
- Rock your pelvis by tilting your pubic bone forward and back (see pages 14–15) a few times to find the mid-point. Remember that the pelvis is the heaviest part of the body and your center of gravity, so make sure it is properly centered. Check that you're not twisting it by holding one hip slightly farther forward than the other.
- Lift your ribs up as far from your hips as you can, so your chest opens out, your shoulders drop down and back and your arms roll slightly outward. Drop your ribs and lift them again a few times so that you can feel the difference. Try to maintain this lift: it will become second nature to you when you have strengthened the muscles of the trunk by practicing the key positions on pages 25–41.
- Pull your shoulders down away from your ears, at the same time lengthening the back of your neck upward.
- Move your nose slightly up and down a few times, so your head rocks back and forth; then balance your head, with the chin at about a right angle to the front of your neck.

With practice, this sequence becomes one rippling movement – pelvic tilt, ribs up, shoulders down and back, back of the neck up – and takes only a couple of seconds. This is the same movement as you'll learn in the relaxation routine on pages 74–6; bad posture is often associated with tension. If you practice this rippling movement a few times a day, the easy, balanced posture shown on the next page will soon become natural to you, enabling you to cope well with the extra weight of the baby. Not only will your whole body function at its best, but it will also look its best, for correct use of the body also means correct sculpturing of its contours.

Bad posture

below left There are as many varieties of bad posture as there are people, but in pregnancy the weight of the baby encourages this particular slouch. If you are not using the abdominal muscle corset and the buttocks to support the growing weight, the curve at the back of the waist becomes over-exaggerated to compensate for the extra weight in front. This squeezes the vertebrae above and below the waist and distorts the whole spine, putting a great burden on it, which usually makes itself felt as pain and stiffness. Because the pelvis is not centered, your thighs, buttocks and abdomen don't work properly, and they tend to become flabby. This can be corrected by doing a pelvic tilt (see pages 14–15) which also lengthens the lower back. Check that the rest of your body is well balanced with the rocking movements and adjustments on page 19.

Help from your partner

below right If you tend to over-arch your back and find it hard to correct, a partner can help you to check that your pelvis is centered, your ribs are lifted and your shoulders are down and relaxed.

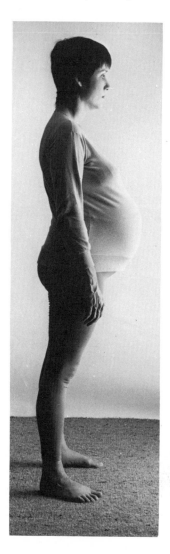

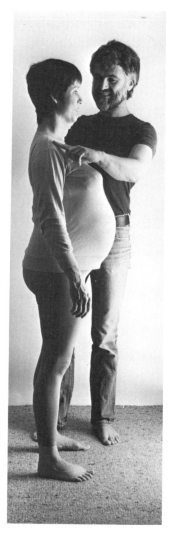

The benefits of good posture

Your ribs and chest lift, so you can expand the rib cage and breathe well. In the last months of pregnancy, this makes you feel less constricted and gives you more space to breathe.

Your abdominal muscles are not allowed to sag, so they act as a strong corset to support the growing weight and soon regain their compact shape after the birth.

The pelvis is correctly positioned, so both the buttocks and the abdomen can help support the trunk effectively, preventing lower back strain.

The back of the neck lengthens upward, so your head is well balanced and doesn't compress your neck or distort your spine.

Your shoulders are dropped, preventing unnecessary tension in the shoulders, neck and the upper back.

Your spine is lengthened, allowing plenty of space to accommodate the baby.

_____*Protecting your spine*_____

The spine is the supporting structure of the body, connecting your head, ribs, pelvis and limbs. Give it the respect it deserves by learning how to safeguard it as you go about your everyday life. This is particularly important in pregnancy because you're not only heavier but your muscles, ligaments and joints are loosened by the extra progesterone in your body.

The essential point is to lengthen your back as much as possible. Between each movable joint of the spine is a soft jelly-like disc that allows great freedom of movement – if you habitually allow your spine to sag, these soft discs may become squashed, causing stiffness and pain. Strength in the muscles of your back, which you can develop by practicing the key positions on pages 25–41, helps you keep the spine lengthened without thinking about it. Mobility of the joints of the spine also helps: if your back is stiff and inflexible, loosen it up with the exercises on pages 48–9.

Lifting, bending and carrying

If you hold yourself well, your spine will be well lifted; give it extra protection by learning to lift, bend and carry without straining your back. Always bend your knees, not your back. This not only protects the delicate joints and discs of the spine but keeps your hip joints mobile and strengthens your thighs. All the forward-bending exercises in this book are done with a straight back, bending from the hips, so that the principle should become second nature to you. It's a matter of re-educating yourself if you've gotten out of the habit – small children always bend in this way. Remember these guidelines to help you keep your back straight and well lifted:

- Bend down into a squat whenever you need to reach down, for example when lifting something from a low cupboard or drawer, or when gardening. Brace your pelvic floor (see the drawbridge exercise on page 13) and abdominal muscles before lifting children or other heavy weights.
- Stand close to any object to be lifted, positioning yourself round it if possible, with one foot forward and one back to give you a broader, more stable base to work from.
- Always face the object to be lifted square on: never pick up something with your body in a twisted position.
- As you lift, bring the weight close in to the pelvis, your center of gravity, as soon as possible.
- When carrying children, change sides often, and try not to twist your body as you hold them (see page 123 for advice on carrying a baby).
- If you have to carry heavy bags, distribute the weight evenly on each side of you, and remember your posture.
- Avoid lifting heavy weights up high or lifting them down from a height. When your arms are raised, your back tends to over-arch and the vertebrae get squeezed; if you add the extra weight of lifting something high, it may be too much for your back.
- Whenever you stretch upward, do a small pelvic tilt (see pages 14–15) before raising your arms to prevent your lower back arching.

If you are pregnant and already have a toddler, you need to protect your back — there's no doubt that it will come under great strain, as it's practically impossible to avoid picking up a young child. So take extra care to bend your knees and keep your back straight when lifting. As often as possible, sit down to cuddle him so you don't have to carry his weight as well as the extra you are carrying with the second pregnancy. A useful trick is to get him to climb onto a steady chair or low table and cuddle or dress him there so you don't have to lift him.

Lying on the floor and standing up

The golden rules are always turn on your side, and always get up slowly, whether you're getting out of bed or up from the floor. This is important in late pregnancy, and at any time if you have a weak back.

To lie down, take a step forward and slowly lower yourself onto one knee, making sure you don't jolt it. Kneel on both knees, sit back on your heels and then shift onto one hip. Lie down on your side and finally roll onto your back, and straighten your legs.

To stand up, reverse the process. Pause for a few moments when you're sitting on one hip to give your circulation time to adjust from lying to the upright position. Use the strength of your thighs to stand up, keeping your trunk upright. If you need a little extra help, put your hands on the raised knee, lean your trunk slightly forward and push yourself up with your hands.

Sitting well and standing up

Don't sit with your legs crossed or, worse, double-crossed with one foot under the other calf, as this twists your back and constricts the circulation in your legs. It's particularly important not to do this if you have varicose veins. Instead, have your thighs supported on the chair, so they can turn slightly outward, and rest your feet on the floor.

To stand up, sit upright, bend forward from your hips and push off with your feet, feeling the thigh muscles work (below right). Keep your neck and back straight and don't allow your chin to jut forward. Practice this, first with one foot in front and then the other, until it becomes a habit.

These positions, together with the pelvic movements on pages 13–18, form the basis of getting your body into good shape for pregnancy and labor. They also build your confidence in your ability to guide your body during labor. For you'll find that, as well as strengthening your muscles, some of the positions give you a considerable stretch – which of them do this and where the stretch comes depend on your particular areas of stiffness. This gives you an opportunity to prepare for coping with the pain of contractions. As you first feel the stretch, become aware of your body's natural response to tension. As you hold the position, breathe rhythmically and calmly – by breathing into the pain, directing your breath toward and not against or away from it, you'll gradually realize that the pain is receding and becoming tolerable. This dynamic combination of breathing, acceptance and then release is an important part of your preparation for labor. Try to hold each position slightly longer each time and so gradually extend your capacity to breathe and release into the stretch. Go through the head-to-toe relaxation on pages 74–5 and, once you're familiar with the routine, focus on keeping your body as relaxed as possible while you hold the key positions. Let your back round to relax it when you've finished.

Practice a little every day to build up your confidence. All the positions are useful for general fitness, so encourage your partner to do them with you. They also have the advantage that:

- You can be your own teacher and see for yourself how you progress. You can correct your mistakes easily, too.
- They can be done at home and fitted into your everyday activities.
- No matter how unfit you are, you can start to improve by using these safe positions.
- They teach you to hold and move your body correctly in everyday life and when doing other exercises, so you're less likely to suffer from backache. If you already suffer from back pain, see page 62 for advice.
- All the positions help you to get used to being on the floor. Floor level is the safest and most convenient when dealing with small children, and the children enjoy being with you at their level instead of always having to look up at you. Also, it does your spine, hips and legs a great deal more good than sitting on sofas and chairs. It's good practice if you intend to have your baby squatting on a bed or on the floor.

Acute pain is always a danger signal. If you find holding the position a great strain, come out of it and try again later, maybe doing a simple variation instead, with more support and props. It's better to hold the position for a few moments doing it well and understanding your aims, than to persist grimly. Gradually you'll be able to hold each one longer, with fewer rests in between, until it becomes a natural position for you: a little regularly should be your motto. If you find it hard to hold the positions, even with calm breathing, get someone to give you firm, slow massage up the spine, as shown on page 85, helping you to lift the spine with each upward stroke. If it's your inside thighs that are feeling particularly uncomfortable, massage them upward with firm strokes from knee to groin, or ask your partner to do it for you.

_____*First strengthen your back*_____

Whichever of the first three key positions you're practicing, it's essential that you try to straighten your back, as this straightening motion strengthens the back muscles. You will probably find this hard at first; these variations on the poses help you develop the strength you need. The instructions apply to all these positions, though they are shown here in the first position – tailor sitting.

Sit upright and lift your ribs away from your hips, so your back lengthens. Lift your chest. Pull your shoulders down, feeling the back of your neck lengthen upward. Hold your chin at about a right angle to the front of your neck. Check that your shoulders are directly above your hips and center your pelvis so you are sitting evenly on both buttocks, and can feel the bones pressing into the floor. Try to hold the position for a few moments but don't let your back become stiff or rigid. Relax and then try again, perhaps holding yourself up a little longer. Don't hold your breath, but breathe slowly and evenly.

At first it's difficult to tell if your back is lifting well or not, so practice the position glancing sideways into a mirror. If you see your back rounding, try to straighten it by lifting the ribs in front a little more. Feel what happens in your body as you do this. You will probably feel the pinch of working muscles for a while somewhere between your shoulder blades and the back of your waist – that's the area that needs strengthening, so you know you are doing the job properly. Check your progress in the mirror every few days until you can keep your ribs lifted and your back straight without discomfort.

left It may help to sit against a wall at first. This is also a good way to tell whether your back is really straight: if you can't feel the length of your spine against the wall, you know it's rounded.

below left If the position seems difficult, sit on one, two or even three cushions or pillows. Aim to make yourself as comfortable as possible, so you can hold the position for a minute at least. As it gets easier you can hold it longer and take away the cushions one by one.

below Prop yourself up with your arms to help you lift. Make a loose fist with each hand and press the fists into the floor behind you as you lift your ribs away from your hips and straighten your back. Don't let your shoulders rise.

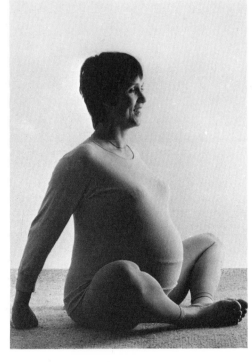

Tailor sitting

WHY This position is useful in preparation for labor as it loosens the groin and hips, and stretches the muscles of the inner thighs. It also stimulates the circulation in the lower half of the body. Practicing this will help you to hold a variety of positions in labor and will help you let your legs flop wide apart during the delivery.

HOW Sit on the floor with the soles of your feet together. Hold your ankles. Bring your pelvis and feet as close together as you can by "walking" forward on your hips. Keep your back straight.

right You may find it helpful to place a couple of cushions under each of your thighs for support.

right To help loosen your hips and thighs, ask a partner to kneel in front of you, hands firmly under your knees. (Make sure she leans forward from the hips with a straight back.) Press your thighs down, asking your partner to resist the push. Repeat this a few times. Afterward, you'll find your legs will drop slightly farther than they did before. You can also do this yourself or, alternatively, lean back on your hands as you pull your thighs down.

left Try this position lying down if it doesn't come easily to you. Place a cushion under your pelvis for comfort in the lower back area, if necessary.

below Sitting cross-legged is a useful variation on this position: remember to change the front leg occasionally.

right Another variation is to have one foot resting on the floor in front of the other. Remember to change feet.

below Once the upright position feels comfortable, try leaning your trunk forward to make your hips more mobile and give an extra stretch in the legs. Breathe in and, as you breathe out, lower yourself forward. Keep your back straight and move from the hips, until you feel a stretch again. Stop and wait for the stretch to subside, breathing well, before going farther. You can also do this in the next key position.

Sitting, legs apart

WHY In common with the first position, this stretches the groin and inside thighs. Both this and the next position stretch the back of the legs. They also strengthen the quadriceps – the muscles at the front of the thighs; as these are the muscles that hold the knees in place and keep them healthy, this is particularly important in pregnancy when the extra weight can put undue strain on the knees. Flexing your feet while you're sitting in these positions strengthens them, which also helps you to cope with the weight of the baby.

HOW Sitting down, move your legs an equal distance apart until you feel a stretch on your inside thighs. Make sure your knees face directly up. Follow the instructions on pages 26–7 to help you straighten your back if you find this difficult. Bend your feet up, pushing away with your heels, so you feel the back of your legs stretching and the front of your thighs tightening.

right To lift your back and stretch your legs, place a scarf or belt round each foot and pull on it gently.

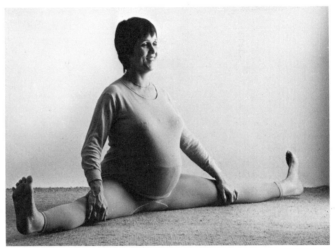

above As the stretch on your thighs subsides, press your hands into the floor behind you, lifting your hips up a little, and bring your hips slightly forward so your legs go a little farther apart. Make sure they're still an equal distance from the center and let your hands relax.

Sitting, legs straight in front

WHY This is a terrific strengthener as it's particularly hard work to keep the back straight and your legs stretched out in front. The body tends to get tense and tight down the back of its length, from the base of the skull to the back of the heels. This position is a good way of stretching and of undoing tightness and tension: it helps to create a strong, supple body. Don't try this if you have sciatica. In late pregnancy, avoid leaning forward in this position, as the growing baby makes this uncomfortable.

HOW Sit with your legs bent, knees and feet together. Lift your back and gradually straighten your legs, pushing your feet away from you along the floor. If your back begins to round, use your hands behind you to help.

above You can help yourself learn this by placing one leg straight out in front, the knee facing the ceiling, with a scarf or belt round the center of the foot. Have the other leg bent and dropping out sideways, a cushion under it for support, if necessary. Bend up the foot of the outstretched leg and push away with the heel. Lift your ribs, gently pulling against the scarf to straighten your back and leg. Repeat on the other side.

Also try putting a scarf round the center of both feet and gently pulling on it to lift and straighten the back. You can do this against a wall for extra support if you need it. Make sure your hips are even and your knees and ankles are level. To make the stretch on the back of the legs stronger, place the scarf round the balls of the feet. This improves the circulation in the back of the calves and strongly stretches the Achilles tendons.

right You can sit like this in a chair as well as on the floor if you prop your feet up roughly level with your hips.

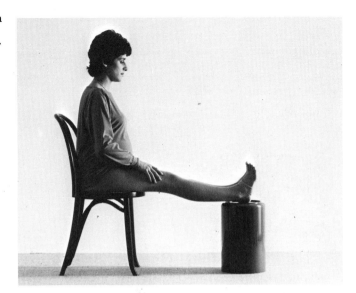

right Putting a few books under your heels also stretches the Achilles tendons and the back of your calves. Use your hands for balance, if necessary,

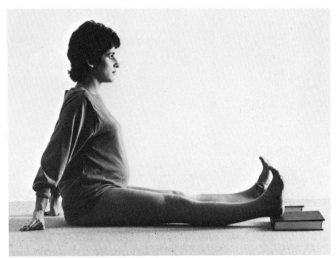

Squatting

WHY You may want to squat in labor –
practicing it beforehand means you won't find
it a strain. Meanwhile it strengthens your
thighs and feet and stretches your Achilles
tendons, calves and inner thigh muscles, all of
which tend to be too tight. Squat whenever
you need to bend to floor level, as bending
your legs protects your back (see page 22).
Always get up slowly, preferably holding on to
a chair or table, or you may feel dizzy.

HOW Squat down, keeping
your back lengthened. If you
can, keep your heels on the
floor and balance your weight
evenly between the balls of
the feet and the heels, not
allowing your feet to roll
inward or outward. Press your
arms against your thighs as
this increases the stretch on
the groin and inside thighs.

right At first, stand with your back against a wall, feet a little way from it, hip-width apart. Slide down the wall until you are in the squatting position. If you feel that your weight is pressing back, keep practicing against the wall and try to bring your weight forward. When you feel quite stable and the position is reasonably comfortable, squat without the support behind you. You may like to use cushions under your bottom for support, whether or not you're leaning against a wall.

below You're more stable in this position if you have a partner to practice with, who can hold your hands. Make sure that your own feet are parallel and that you're facing each other directly.

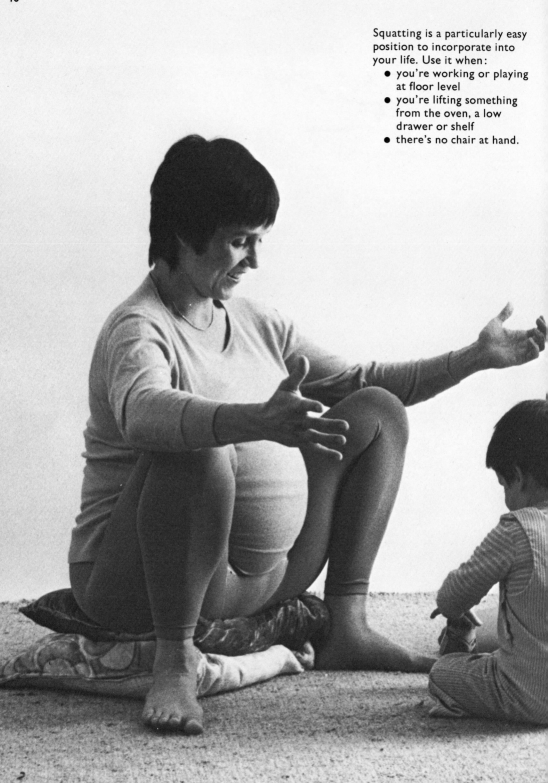

Squatting is a particularly easy
position to incorporate into
your life. Use it when:
- you're working or playing
  at floor level
- you're lifting something
  from the oven, a low
  drawer or shelf
- there's no chair at hand.

Now that you're familiar with the essential pelvic exercises and key positions, you can begin to judge for yourself which are your weak areas. As you go through your day try to estimate truthfully how your body feels, and where you need to be stronger. Which parts of you tire easily or get stiff? Don't brush away the warning signs. Instead be positive – write them down if you find this helpful. Then go through this section and make up a daily program of movements to tone up the areas that need help *before* the twinge or tiredness turns into an ache or pain. If you've already developed aches or pains, turn to pages 60–3 for advice. None of the movements requires special equipment – just make sure your clothes are comfortable. Don't go on exercising so long that you're exhausted and stop if you feel any sudden pain.

Neck and shoulders

This is an area where everyone gathers a lot of tension. It's a useful barometer for how you're coping with stress and strains, if you know how to read it. The following movements and the massage on pages 85 and 90 show you how to

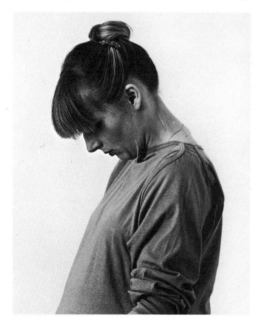 

above left Pull your shoulders down, breathing in, and lengthen the back of your neck upward. As you breathe out, draw your chin in and lower your head forward, until you feel a stretch in the back of your neck, and maybe down your back as well. Take a few breaths, breathing out slowly and completely. As you do this, you'll feel the stretch easing. If it doesn't, you're dropping your head too far – so come up a little. If it's easy, gently take your head farther down, allowing your back

to round. Breathe calmly; breathe in as you slowly lift your head.

above right Breathe in, pulling your shoulders down and lengthening the back of your neck upward. As you breathe out, tilt your head back about halfway. Don't drop it right back so you're facing the ceiling, as you'll compress the neck joints. Hold as before, breathe in and raise your head. Now combine the forward and backward tilts.

become aware of the tension in your neck and shoulders long before it has turned into discomfort or even pain. Moving your head in all directions daily and stroking the back of your neck and shoulders give you a feeling of well-being, and make the whole area feel light and free. They also help prevent tension headaches and waking with a stiff neck or frozen shoulder. While practicing your head and shoulder movements, try not to tense up other areas of your body; it's especially important to keep your face and shoulders relaxed (see page 75 for advice on how to do this).

Neck

This part of the spine is delicately designed to give it great freedom of movement, so treat it with the care and respect it deserves and never jerk your neck as you exercise it. Practice each movement once: don't worry if you hear a lot of creaks as you move, as your neck and shoulders will soon become healthier and more flexible. Don't circle your head round in one continuous movement, as this puts a lot of strain on the neck joints.

above left Draw in your chin and tilt your head to the left, facing forward. Hold as before, feeling a stretch on the right side of your neck. Bring your head up and repeat to the right.

above right Turn your head to face diagonally to the right. Draw in your chin and lower your head. If the stretch is not too much, lower your head farther and round your back. Hold for a few moments and slowly lift your head; return to the center and repeat to the left.

right Turn your head to face right, looking round, which will help you turn farther. Hold the position for a few moments and repeat to the left.

Shoulders

Most work requires your hands to be forward in your field of vision. This means that your neck, shoulders and upper back may slump forward as well, encouraging permanently rounded shoulders. This is particularly undesirable in pregnancy, when you need as much space at the front of your body as possible. You can counteract this forward slump by pulling your shoulders back and opening your chest with these backward shoulder circles and stretches.

below Hold your arms straight out at shoulder level and make a loose fist with each hand. Pull your shoulder blades together and press your arms back in strong, short movements, pressing your chest slightly forward at the same time. Don't let your arms drop.

right Put your hands on your ribs. Let them move as you pull your elbows together behind you. Try to get your elbows to touch. Repeat with several sharp pulls back.

below Clasp your hands behind you, fingers interlocking, elbows bent. Keep your elbows bent as you pull them together behind you, so you get a good squeeze between the shoulder blades and open out your chest.

right Place your fingertips on your shoulders and make large backward circles with your elbows. You can also do backward shoulder circles with your arms at your sides or with your arms outstretched.

left Try this for a stretch between your shoulder blades and a change from the backward pulling movements when you're doing the whole sequence. Clasp your hands, fingers interlocking. Stretch your arms out in front, palms facing away from you; hold for a few moments.

Breasts

Your breasts are likely to become larger and heavier during pregnancy, and unless you support them with a well-fitting bra, they may sag and lose their shape. So even if you don't normally wear a bra, you should do so while your breasts are heavier. There are no muscles in the breasts themselves but you can help to maintain their shape by exercising the muscle underneath. If you practice this exercise naked, you'll see it working.

Make a loose fist with one hand and clasp the other round it. Hold your hands level with your breasts and press your hands together tightly for a few moments. Do the same at eye level and waist level; repeat the sequence several times. Change hands occasionally.

Abdomen

Strong abdominal muscles help you carry the baby more easily, without straining your back. They are also helpful during the birth, when the baby is being pushed out, and of course the better the condition of your muscles the easier it is to restore them afterward.

The most important exercise for the abdominal muscles is simply to pull in your abdomen as you breathe out, as often as you can. You can do this with or without doing a pelvic tilt first (see pages 14–15): practice both, in any position. Bracing your muscles like this helps you cope with the extra weight and it's safe whether or not the muscles have separated (see below). You can also practice the curl down on page 112 throughout pregnancy, except perhaps during the last few weeks if you get very large. If your muscles are in good condition and you were used to doing curl ups (see page 113) before your pregnancy, continue as long as they're not uncomfortable. Just remember not to strain – if you feel pressure on the pelvic floor, the exercise is too strenuous.

It's important to check that the muscles running down the length of the abdomen haven't separated outward because of the pregnancy and, if they have, to work on preventing the condition worsening. Before your abdomen begins to enlarge, check for separation by feeling for a gap between the muscles, as on pages 110–11. During the last six months or so, follow the method below.

above Lie on your back with your legs bent, feet hip-width apart; support your head and shoulders on two cushions. Place the fingers of one hand below your navel. Breathe in; as you breathe out, tuck in your chin and slowly lift your head and shoulders. If your muscles have separated, you'll feel a bulge of flesh below the navel, between the taut muscles.

above To strengthen the muscles, lift your head and shoulders as before, breathing out as you do so, but this time cross your arms over your abdomen to support it and to pull it in toward the center. If your abdomen begins to bulge you have come up too far; lower yourself back a little. Hold the position for a few moments, pulling in the abdomen and pressing your right hand to the right and your left hand to the left. Breathe in as you lower your head and shoulders. Repeat three times, twice a day. You can do these curl ups in bed if you prefer. If you find it very difficult to raise your head and shoulders, place one, two or even three pillows under your head to help you; take away one pillow at a time.

If you're holding yourself well, with a lengthened spine, and practicing the key positions, your back muscles will be growing stronger. It's also important to maintain flexibility – try these exercises if your back is stiff or if you find lengthening your back in the key positions hard. Gently twisting your back is relaxing and invigorating and helps to prevent you straining it with a sudden turn. Stretch out your back with a pelvic tilt (see pages 14–15) before you start. If you already have back pain, turn to page 62 for guidance.

left It's easiest to avoid over-arching your spine if you do this stretch sitting, but you can also do it standing or lying down. Practice the movement sitting against a wall. Pull your shoulder blades together and down, and drop your chin a little. As you do the pelvic tilt, press your back against the wall for a few moments. Get into the habit of practicing this whenever you settle into a chair or car seat.

below left Once you have the knack, stretch your arms above your head at the same time, flattening them as far back as you can against the wall. Keep your shoulders down.

below For an extra stretch, reach up with each arm alternately.

top First try the twist kneeling, as your thighs are anchored and prevent your hips twisting too. Kneel with your knees hip-width apart. Slowly twist to the right, looking round; hold for a moment, then repeat to the left.

above You can press against your knee to help you twist farther if you sit cross-legged.

right Swing your arms for extra momentum as you twist from side to side standing up. Check that both knees remain facing forward.

The buttocks play an essential part in supporting the trunk and the growing weight of the baby as, together with the abdominal muscles, they control the tilt of your pelvis. As the abdominal muscles become stretched because of the growing bulge in front, you depend more on your buttocks to keep correct posture and prevent low back pain. Strong buttocks may also help to prevent sciatica. If they are flabby and collect a lot of fat, or if they protrude at the sides of your thighs, you can take it that they need strengthening.

The simplest exercise is to squeeze your buttocks together as though you were trying to hold a bank note between them. Do some slow squeezes, holding the buttocks together for the count of five, then do some quick ones.

below This exercise is particularly effective, as your buttocks are held in tightly. Lie on your back with your legs bent, feet hip-width apart. Do a pelvic tilt (see pages 14–15) and continue pushing your hips up until your back is in a straight line from shoulders to knees. Don't lift any higher than this or you'll over-arch your back. Hold the position for a few moments, squeezing your buttocks tightly together. Lower your hips, passing through the pelvic tilt position again to stretch out the lower back. Repeat three times, twice a day. You can also do this exercise when you are resting on the floor with your legs up on a low sofa or bed, keeping your legs straight, as on page 57. Once you're used to it, try practicing the drawbridge exercise (see page 13) at the same time.

right To flex your back and work your abdomen as well as strengthening the buttocks, twist your hips from side to side while they are lifted. It's the same movement as the twist with a towel on page 18.

above For a stretch in the buttocks. Lie on your back. Keeping your shoulders and right leg on the floor, bend your left knee and cup the heel in your right hand. Hold your left knee with your left hand. Hold the left heel in toward your groin and bring your left knee toward your left shoulder until you feel a stretch in the left buttock. Repeat with the right leg.

Legs and feet

Unless your legs and feet are strong, the extra weight you're carrying makes them very tired. Strong muscles help to prevent cramps and encourage good circulation – if you've been sitting down for too long, these exercises will make your legs feel less sluggish. If you have varicose veins, stimulating the blood flow is particularly helpful (see also page 63). Most women have over-tight muscles at the

below For the quadriceps. Stand well, with your feet together. Have your fingertips touching a wall or table for balance. Rise up onto the balls of your feet. Do a pelvic tilt (see pages 14–15), clenching your buttocks tightly together; bend your knees, letting them part. Do several more small bends until you're tired. Stand up straight.

below To strengthen the calf muscles. Stand well, fingertips touching a wall for balance. Rise up onto the balls of your feet. Lower your heels halfway down to the floor and lift them well up again. Repeat several times until your calves begin to feel tired. Stand up straight and shake out your legs when you've finished the exercise.

back of their calves, especially if they wear high-heeled shoes. As this inhibits circulation, you should stretch these muscles regularly. It's also important to exercise the quadricep muscles at the front of the thighs: they encase the knee joints, so they must be strengthened in order to keep your knees in good condition. Take your shoes off while practicing these, and preferably do them in bare feet — just walking barefoot helps to strengthen your feet.

left To stretch the tendons at the back of the calves and ankles. Stand with your feet together. Balance yourself with your fingertips on a wall, if necessary. Step forward with one leg, bending the knee. Try to press the back heel down onto the floor. Let it come up and press down again several times. If it's easy, move your legs farther apart. Repeat with the other leg in front. Use this lunging forward position when vacuuming or sweeping — it helps to protect your back as well as stretching your legs.

left For flexibility of hips and legs. Stand well, your right hand against a wall. Do a small pelvic tilt and maintain it throughout. Gently swing your left leg out sideways and then across your body, brushing the foot along the floor in between. Make the swing gentle and easy: don't lift your leg higher than 45°. Do this up to six times; turn round and repeat with your right leg. Now swing each leg forward and back. Repeat as before.

right and far right For the quadriceps. Sit forward on a chair or stool. Do a pelvic tilt and maintain it. Lift one leg, bend it a little and straighten it, pushing away with the heel so the muscle above the knee tightens strongly. Repeat several times slowly and then more quickly. Change to the other leg.

below To stretch the back of your legs and help prevent and cure cramps. Sit with your legs out in front. Ask your partner to lift one leg and hold the heel in one hand and then to press your toes toward you with the other hand until you feel a stretch. Repeat a few times and change legs.

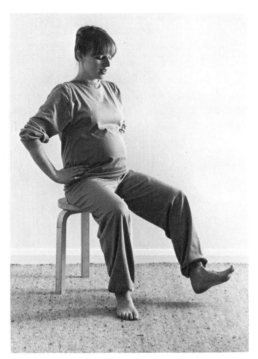

right To strengthen and stretch the ankles. Sit well. Move your feet slightly forward, lift the toes and bring them together. Brush your feet along the floor turning them out and lifting the little toes up as far as you can, as you press the big toes down. Then brush your feet along the floor to return to the first position. Repeat until you begin to tire.

right To strengthen the feet. Sit well and move your feet forward. Lift your toes as far as you can, keeping your heels on the floor. Clench your toes and then stretch them out as far as you can. Repeat several times.

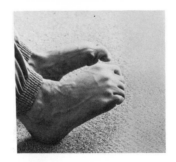

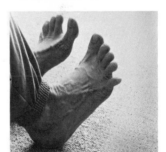

right To strengthen the arches of the feet, put your toes on a thick book and lift the balls of your feet off the floor. Repeat several times.

Plenty of rest and sleep are essential during pregnancy. But there may be times when you have to delay proper rest and this is when the ten minute pick-me-up can be a useful standby. Use it whenever you need to – it wards off tiredness in your lower back, hips and legs, and makes you feel better all over.

Take your shoes off and make sure your clothes are loose and comfortable. Lie on the floor or on a bed where you can put your feet up on a wall. If you're on the floor, you could also rest your feet on a sofa or armchair. Put a cushion or two under your pelvis if you find this more comfortable.

1 Lie on your back. Bend both legs and rest your feet, one by one, on the wall about 2 ft above your heart, no higher. Straighten your legs. Shut your eyes, take a few deep breaths and relax for about three minutes.

2 Bring your feet down the wall a little, bending your knees. Pushing off with your feet, do a pelvic tilt (see pages 14–15), tightening your buttocks and abdomen. Repeat the tilt a few times, practicing the drawbridge exercise for your pelvic floor at the same time (see page 13).

3 Straighten your legs and push up with your hips, so your body forms a straight line from shoulders to feet. Hold for a few moments, clenching your buttock muscles. Repeat a few times.

4 Roll your pelvis from side to side. Lie with your legs slightly bent, hips on the floor or bed, feet on the wall. Push off from the wall with your right foot, rolling to the left; straighten the right leg completely and tighten the right buttock as you roll. Then reverse, rolling to the right. Repeat a few times. Bring your legs down one at a time, bending them as you do so.

5 Bring the soles of the feet together and let your thighs drop outward, into the tailor position (see page 28). Rub your inside thighs as you rest for a minute or so.

6 If the tailor position is easy, straighten your legs up on the wall again, move them apart and hold them there for a while. You can massage your inside thighs in this position too, to ease aching legs.

Finally, take three slow breaths, tightening your abdomen on the out breath. Turn on your side and slowly get up (see page 24). Do a pelvic tilt and have a big stretch when you're up.

In the past, when women became pregnant, they were often treated like invalids and consequently behaved as such. They were forbidden to carry out their normal activities and, after an often traumatic delivery, were kept in bed for two weeks. Small wonder that their list of aches and pains was longer and more serious than ours. Now this has changed: pregnancy is no longer regarded as an illness – if you take sensible care of yourself, you may actually feel better than usual while pregnant. But for some people it's still a time when every twinge makes them worry and when the odd pain can take on a disproportionate importance.

Pregnancy is a good time to increase your body awareness; it should not become a period of constant worrying. A good way to avoid this is to build up a regular exercise program that's well integrated into your everyday life. The self-confidence you'll develop – emotional as well as physical – will enable you to cope with your aches and pains and to keep them in their proper perspective. At the same time you'll be better equipped to recognize a serious problem if one should arise. Remember that the first priority for feeling your best is to make sure that your diet is healthy and that you're getting enough exercise, sleep and relaxation; for further reading on caring for yourself, see page 126. A deep, warm bath can often soothe away tiredness and tension, as well as giving you a chance to appreciate your changing shape.

Don't take any medication, even aspirin, without checking first with your doctor. Always ask for advice on problems that are persistent or troubling, but don't be afraid to help yourself as well. It's never too late to start tackling aches and pains, and you are your own best adviser on what makes you feel better. Taking responsibility for your body now will help you to feel ready for labor and to participate actively in the birth.

————Headaches and tension in the neck————
Tension in the neck is often caused by holding your neck incorrectly and by tense, raised shoulders. You may be unaware of these postural faults until you begin to feel uncomfortable. Pull your shoulders down and the back of your neck will lengthen upward; try to maintain this good posture through the day. Ask your partner to point out when your shoulders are lifted and after a while you'll automatically correct yourself. Practice the neck and shoulder exercises on pages 42–5 every day as well.

If you suffer from tension headaches, ask your partner to massage your neck, shoulders and face (see pages 83–5) or give yourself a massage (see pages 88–90). If these headaches are severe or persist during your pregnancy, go to see your doctor for advice.

————Pain between the shoulders————
Again, this is usually due to tension and the typical bad posture of pregnancy – an arched back and tense shoulders. See pages 19–20 for advice on correcting your balance. Think of your shoulders widening out and dropping down, while you adjust your pelvis. To help yourself become aware of holding your shoulders well, lift them up to your ears and drop them down, pulling toward your feet; repeat twice. Do a few backward shoulder circles afterward to help release any remaining knots of tension.

————Swollen hands————
Many pregnant women wake up with slightly puffy hands, but this generally disappears when they begin to move about. If you're troubled by this, take off any tight rings before you go to sleep. Circle your hands from the wrist, flap them up and down and stretch your fingers out regularly to stimulate your circulation. If the swelling persists, report it to your doctor.

————Tension or pain in the chest————
Pain under the rib cage can be caused by the growing baby pressing the ribs out. Lift your rib cage up and outward to give yourself the maximum space for breathing comfortably.

The expanding uterus
As the baby grows, the intestines and the organs within the pelvic cavity are pushed up and back to make room for the uterus. The womb also presses down on your bladder, so it's no wonder that you need to go to the toilet so often.

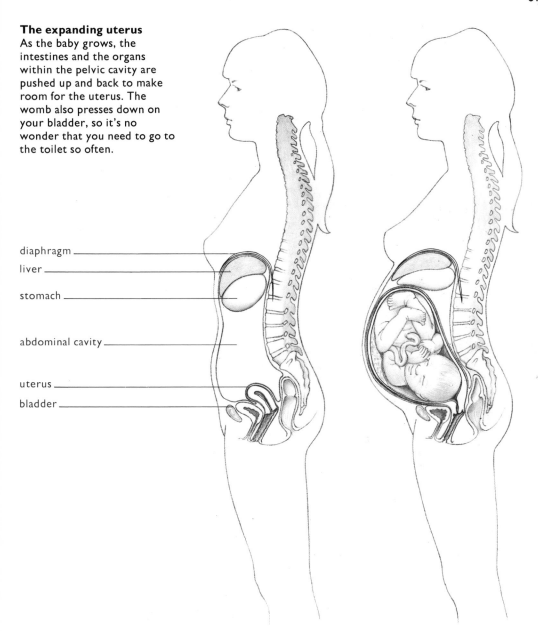

diaphragm

liver

stomach

abdominal cavity

uterus

bladder

Gentle stroking where it hurts can be helpful. To help yourself relax, try resting your fingertips in the middle of the flat space just above your breasts and, breathing out, gently smooth outward with your fingertips to the edge of your shoulders. Breathe in as you bring your fingers in to the center and repeat. Also try the exercise on page 44, your hands on your ribs.

When your baby's head drops, or engages, in preparation for birth, you'll probably find this pain disappears. This usually happens at about 36 weeks with a first baby, although there can be a great deal of variation. With subsequent pregnancies, however, it may not happen until a few days before delivery or even until your labor has already started.

Heartburn

This is a common complaint that seems to be most noticeable toward the end of pregnancy. Increased production of the hormone progesterone slackens the muscle tone of the gastrointestinal tract and allows the reflux of gastric juices into the esophagus, causing the burning sensation. It's better not to get too tired and hungry before eating, and to eat slowly. Try eating small snacks every two hours and don't have your main meal too late at night.

More rest and good posture help: lift your spine, making as much space between your pelvis and ribs as possible. Do the exercises to strengthen your abdomen on pages 46–7. Try sleeping with an extra pillow, or prop the head of your bed up slightly on a few books.

Morning sickness

This can be extremely unpleasant and debilitating, but it usually passes by the 14th week of pregnancy. Unfortunately, there are no exercises that help to relieve it, but you can help yourself by eating frequent small meals and drinking plenty of fluids. If you're out for long periods, carry some hard candy in your handbag. Sweet tea and a dry cookie or toast eaten 20 minutes before you get up in the morning often help. Consult your doctor before taking any medication – there are drugs available that in some cases can alleviate this condition.

Braxton-Hicks contractions

These are "practice" contractions of the uterus that are usually most noticeable toward the end of pregnancy; they're particularly common after orgasm. They are quite normal but can occasionally cause a little pain, which gives you a good opportunity to practice your relaxation and breathing for labor (see pages 74–6 and 79–80). Try the very light fingertip massage on page 91 as well.

Backache

This is one of the most common problems of pregnancy – your back is vulnerable because of the extra progesterone, which softens the ligaments supporting the spine. If you already have any back problems, you should be particularly careful when you are pregnant. Read the section on pages 22–4 on protecting your spine and remember to bend your knees when lifting anything heavy.

Bad posture is the most likely cause of general discomfort in the back. So begin by checking your posture against the illustrations on pages 20–1; and do pelvic tilts regularly (see pages 14–15). You may find moving in water helpful, particularly the stretching and floating exercises shown on page 69.

If you are in pain, stop whatever you are doing – pain is always a warning signal and should not be disregarded. Squat for a minute or two and then lie down, lying on your side before you turn onto your back. It's best to lie on a firm surface – on the floor if you are comfortable and warm, or on a firm bed. Put one small cushion under your head and another under your hips; relax your shoulders, arms and hands. Bend your legs, do a pelvic tilt and press your back into the floor – check that you are managing this by slipping one hand between your back and the floor. If there's still space between them, rest your hips on another pillow or two to lengthen out your lower back.

When you are well supported, take two or three slow breaths, relaxing into the floor on each out breath. When the pain has subsided, roll onto your side, sit for a minute and then slowly stand up. You may find that massage helps – ask your partner to try the strokes for the back shown on page 85.

Once you are free of pain, start exercising. The key positions on pages 25–41 are excellent for strengthening the back. Frequent backache may be caused by weak abdominal muscles, leaving your back to do more than its fair share of the work, so look also at the exercises to strengthen the abdomen on pages 46–7.

Two minute routine for backache
- Forward pelvic tilt (see pages 14–15)
- Side to side tilting (see page 16)
- Circling your hips all round (see page 16)
- Twisting your hips (see page 18)
- Twisting your shoulders (see page 49).

Sciatica

Once again, extra progesterone may be the culprit in pregnancy for this pain, felt in the sciatic nerve, running from the lower back through the buttocks and down the back of the legs. Find time for extra rest, lying on your side with a pillow between your thighs. Exercise gently: stand and slowly swing each leg back, as on page 54. The exercises on pages 50–1 for the buttocks are helpful for sciatica, especially bending one leg up as you lie on the floor – if it's your right buttock that hurts, bend up your right leg, and vice versa.

_____Shooting pain in the legs_____
Sudden shooting pain in your groin or down one leg when you walk is probably due to pressure from the baby. Stop and rest, breathing slowly until the pain goes away. Take more rest: have a nap every day, or at least lie down or sit with your feet up for an hour every day.

_____Pressure in the vagina_____
Pressure from the baby dropping low down into the pelvis as you near the birth day can be uncomfortable. Squatting can help; practice the drawbridge exercise on page 13 as you squat.

_____Constipation_____
Extra progesterone relaxes the muscles of the gut so that they work less efficiently and this may cause constipation. Eat more fiber (bran or raw fruits and vegetables, for example) and drink lots of water. Iron pills may aggravate the condition; ask your doctor to change your brand of pill or try you on a lower dosage.

Never strain or hold your breath on the toilet. The squatting position may be a help – raise your feet by resting them on a box or low table, or squat over a pot. Contract and release your pelvic floor (see page 13) several times to stimulate the muscles. Release your pelvic floor as you have a bowel movement and breathe out slowly as you gently push.

_____Incontinence_____
The bulk of the uterus pressing down on the pelvic floor leaves little space for your bladder, so it's normal to empty your bladder often. If you leak a little urine when you sneeze or cough, it's a warning signal that your pelvic floor needs strengthening. This condition can often be prevented or cured by regular practice of the drawbridge exercise on page 13. Like all muscles, those of the pelvic floor need to be exercised regularly in order to keep them in good condition.

_____Varicose veins_____
The extra progesterone in your body relaxes the muscle in the walls of your veins, increasing the risk of varicose veins developing. These can appear in the legs or in the vulva (the opening of the vagina) or in the anal passage, where they are called hemorrhoids. If you have hemorrhoids, take care to avoid constipation and straining. Go to your doctor for advice or medication as, if neglected, hemorrhoids can be extremely painful.

Varicose veins usually subside after the baby is born, but they do tend to return with each pregnancy. Some women are more prone to them than others, but everyone can take measures to try to prevent them appearing. Never sit with your legs crossed (see page 24) and whenever you can, sit or lie with your feet up. Don't stand if you can sit, or sit if you can lie down, and make sure you rest every day. Circle your ankles as often as possible to aid your circulation and fit in as much brisk walking and swimming as you can. The key positions on pages 25–41 and the exercises for legs and feet on pages 52–5 are also useful.

Don't wear any tight elastic round your legs. If you wear support stockings, rest your feet up against a wall as you lie in bed and put on the stockings before you stand up.

_____Aching legs_____
Again, try to rest with your feet up, and never stand still for longer than you have to. Do some exercise as well – swimming and walking are both excellent. Gentle massage up the legs may help, as may practicing the key positions on pages 25–41.

_____Cramps_____
These can be very painful and annoying if they wake you up in the middle of the night. There's no proven remedy, but you might try a calcium and Vitamin D supplement, or extra milk.

If you get cramps in your calf muscles, sit in the position on page 35, with a scarf round the ball of the foot on the side with the cramp. Pull the ball of the foot firmly toward you until the cramp subsides. Better still, ask a friend to do this for you, as on page 54. Both exercises help to prevent cramps as well.

If the cramps are in your foot, bend it upward. When the cramps subside, do some ankle circles to stimulate the circulation. Massage can be comforting too (see pages 87 and 91). As a preventive measure, do the key positions and the exercises for feet on page 55.

_____Swollen legs and ankles_____
Some women suffer from swollen ankles during pregnancy, especially in hot weather. Flat, comfortable shoes help – try not to wear high heels too often. Rest with your feet up as often as possible, use the key positions and try the exercises for the legs and feet on pages 52–5. If your ankles are still puffy, check with your doctor that there's nothing to worry about.

As well as strengthening and loosening your body with indoor exercises and good posture, you'll feel better if you do some regular exercise out of doors. A period of sustained exercise every day keeps your heart and lungs healthy and gets your circulation going.

The best outdoor exercise for a pregnant woman is walking. Whenever you have a choice between walking and driving, take the opportunity to exercise your whole body, rather than just your accelerator foot. Of course, walking in the country is more appealing, with the added attraction of fresh, clean air. But city walking is good for you too, especially if you can include a detour through a park or public garden.

Be aware of your whole body, observing and correcting your posture as you move. Use the opportunity to breathe well, lifting your chest and dropping your shoulders, so you can breathe deeply with no tension. As your pregnancy advances, you may find that when you walk you have a dragging, heavy feeling as the baby presses down on your pelvic floor. This can be alleviated by pulling up your pelvic floor muscles, as in the drawbridge exercise on page 13. Repeat this whenever you think of it.

How long you walk for depends on how you feel. The right clothes and shoes are important so you can relax and enjoy yourself. Wear loose clothes, and flat shoes that give adequate support. You won't tire as quickly if your feet are really comfortable. Start with half an hour a day and work up to longer periods if it suits you. If you enjoy it, you'll naturally find yourself looking for reasons to walk more; if not, find a different way to get fresh air and exercise.

Which other form of exercise you choose depends on your normal exercise routine. Pregnancy is not the ideal time to take up an energetic new sport, but if you regularly jogged, played tennis or squash before you became pregnant, you can normally continue to do so, providing you feel like it. Be especially careful in early pregnancy when hormonal changes affect ligament and muscle tone and ask your doctor's advice on when to stop. If you cycled regularly, you'll probably want to continue as long as you feel confident, but remember that your balance changes a great deal during pregnancy, as your center of gravity alters. Moving in water, including swimming if you can, is an excellent and safe way of working your whole body.

The exercise you do should be relaxing, invigorating and enjoyable, and not too strenuous. Don't push yourself and avoid sudden movements – if you listen to your body you'll know when to stop. The changes pregnancy brings make it impossible to demand as much of yourself as you did before. Relax and respect these changes now – soon enough you'll have had your baby and will be able to resume your normal sporting activities.

Movements in water

All through pregnancy your baby feels rocked in the cradle of your pelvis, floating in her own pool of amniotic liquid. This cushions her from the outside world by filtering sounds and smoothing out the bumps as you move. Everyone's earliest awareness must be of floating; so it's hardly surprising that most people find it easy to relax in, or near, water.

During labor, you may enjoy spending some time in a tub of warm water to help you relax and soothe away tension. While you are pregnant, moving in water can be a pleasure, both as an aid to relaxation and well-being and as a way of exercising safely: in late pregnancy, the support and freedom that the water gives you are particularly enjoyable. Moving slowly and savoring the feeling of the water on your body as you breathe slowly and deeply build up your confidence and strength. These movements can include swimming, but need not. Just being in warm water, floating and stretching to explore the feelings and sensations, is satisfying for swimmers and nonswimmers alike. All the movements shown here, except the floating sequence, can be done even if you can't swim, as they're almost all done at the shallow end of the pool. You should have someone with you though in case you get into difficulties.

If you do prefer swimming, take care not to arch your back as you do so. If you have any back trouble, it's probably best to avoid breaststroke, unless you normally do the glide with your head in the water, since keeping your head up tends to make your lower back over-arch. Try swimming on your back, with breaststroke leg movements, arms mirroring the leg movements, or use side or back stroke if you prefer, but do swim slowly and don't force yourself.

Warm-up

left Stride across the pool at the shallow end. Take giant steps, lifting each leg high and stretching it out in front of you as you walk. Stretch the opposite arm over your head and forward with each step. Breathe deeply and slowly with the movements, building up a good rhythm. Go back and forth a few times.

below Stand with your feet apart, with your arms outstretched at shoulder level on the water. Stretch one arm up over your head, bend it toward the other and try to touch it. Enjoy the stretch along your side. Sway over to the other side. Do two or three good stretches each way.

Rail exercises

right Turn your back to the rail and hold it with your arms outstretched. Raise your legs so you're floating on your back. Move your legs as if bicycling, bending and stretching them slowly through the water, for about two minutes.

right Stand with your back to the rail, holding on. Keeping your back pressed against the side, slide your legs apart, so your body sinks down into the water, and then bring them together again. Repeat four or five times.

below Holding the rail in the same way, stretch your legs straight out in front of you. Bend them up, relaxing into the squatting position. Then move your legs out to the sides as far as possible, feeling the inner thighs stretch, before you bring your legs together again. Make the sequence into one flowing movement and repeat several times.

left Turn to face the rail and, holding onto it, lift your legs up to each side. Slowly move from side to side, keeping your feet flat against the edge.

below Hold the rail, with your arms stretched out in front of you. Lift your legs up behind you, so that you're floating on the water. Kick alternate legs straight up and down, for about two minutes; breathe deeply and rhythmically as you move your legs.

below Holding the rail, move toward the deep end until you're just out of your depth. Still facing the edge, gently swing your legs from side to side, bending from the waist. Repeat ten times. Try this with your back to the rail. Return to the shallow end.

right and below Hold onto the rail and squat against the side. Swing from side to side a few times and return to the center. Take a deep breath and push off backward. As you glide, let your breath out slowly and stretch your body into a straight line, or a star, paddling with your arms if you like.

Floating
below To help yourself float, take a deep breath and lift your body by pushing your pelvis up so you're lying flat on your back on the water. Breathe out slowly; then try to float while breathing normally. You may find it helpful to use a float between your legs or under your pelvis or head.

For every couple, pregnancy opens up new possibilities for sex and love-making. It's the ideal time to learn more about your own and your partner's body, not only through intercourse, but by exploring each other as whole sexual beings. Many women become more relaxed and sensuous in the second half of their pregnancy; this heightened sensuality comes partly from hormonal changes but also from the emotional contentment that being pregnant often brings. You and your partner can enjoy a new variety of sexual expression during pregnancy, trying out new ways of loving and pleasing each other. Sexuality at its most enjoyable involves the development of another, richer language between two people: a vocabulary to which all the senses – touch, sight, smell, hearing and taste – contribute.

Problems and solutions

Some doctors advise couples not to have sexual intercourse at the very beginning or the end of pregnancy. If you have had any bleeding or a threatened miscarriage, it's wise to follow this advice; but always ask when you can start again. It's important that you know whether it is orgasm or intercourse that has to be stopped, or both. If it's intercourse that's not allowed, you can still reach orgasm through oral sex and manual stimulation. If you've been told not to have intercourse or orgasm, remember that you and your partner need to give each other extra love and tenderness during this time.

You may find that in the first three months of pregnancy you feel sick and tired and perhaps don't want intercourse at all. If so, reassure your partner that it's temporary and find other ways to be close with each other. In the last few weeks of pregnancy, you may become troubled by the Braxton-Hicks contractions that can start after having an orgasm. They are harmless to both mother and baby, but if they go on for long, ask your doctor's advice (see also page 62).

Some pregnant women find it hard to adjust to the changes in their bodies, especially when they start to lose their normal shape. They feel fat and unlovable. Try to think positively about your expanding roundness and the life that's growing within you. A sensitive partner who can enjoy and appreciate the changes pregnancy brings to a woman's body can make all the difference.

Pregnancy can also arouse conflicting feelings for men. Pride at their potency may be mixed with apprehension at the changes and extra responsibilities on the way. Some men have fears about sexual intercourse during pregnancy, worrying that penetration may somehow harm the baby, or feeling that the woman's body has become sacred or too fragile for sex. In fact, normal intercourse cannot harm your baby. A plug of mucus at the mouth of the uterus effectively seals off the baby from any infection from the vagina and while external pressure on the abdomen may be uncomfortable for the mother, the baby is well cushioned by amniotic fluid.

Positions during pregnancy

You may find it easier to reach orgasm in the later stages of pregnancy. This is because there's an increase in blood flow causing engorgement of the genitals, similar to the normal non-pregnant state of sexual arousal. However, as your abdomen grows, you'll probably want to adapt your usual positions. For instance, you may find the man-on-top position uncomfortable. You can still use it if your partner supports his weight on his arms so he doesn't press down on your abdomen at all. You may also like to try the "spoons" position, in which you lie on your side, with your partner lying behind you and entering from behind. This is a good position for him to stroke your breasts and clitoris. If you lie on top, you can support your weight on your arms and you have the advantage that you can control the angle and speed of movement of the penis and so reach your orgasm when you want. Your partner can also caress your breasts. Another position that avoids pressure on your abdomen is kneeling on all fours with your head down on your arms. Your partner kneels behind you and enters from behind. In this position you may find that you like your partner to give your clitoris extra stimulation.

Touching and comfort

Even if one or other of you is not in the mood for intercourse, it's always possible to give each other pleasure and comfort. Men and women of all ages need to be lovingly cuddled and held throughout their lives, although some men find this difficult to acknowledge even to themselves and prefer to see this need solely in terms of their sex drive.

Many women experience an increased desire to be held and touched during their pregnancy. There is a good reason for this: a woman who is used to communicating through touch will find it easier to establish loving contact with her baby at birth. Most women sometimes prefer to be held and caressed rather than have intercourse. A woman also needs to feel confident that her man can wait, holding and touching her lovingly in his arms while her passion is aroused. Then often, after their love-making, it is her turn to enfold him, stroking and touching as they relax together. This kind of holding is important for every couple. But for the pregnant couple it has a specific role to play as you prepare for the birth. The more confident you are in expressing affection for your partner, the more fluent your responses will be toward your baby.

For many women, pregnancy, childbirth and the experience of breastfeeding all contribute to a deepened awareness of themselves. They become more attuned to their bodies and feel freer to express their sexuality. This maturity sometimes shows itself slowly but it's worth waiting for the joy it brings. Remember that you are first a couple; pregnancy is a wonderful part of the expression of your love, but it's only a part. Nurture each other in every way – continually affirm your relationship and this will give you the strength and happiness to sustain the family that you are both creating.

Sex and induction

If you know that you are going to be induced, you may like to try to start the labor yourselves by having intercourse. The hormone prostaglandin is found in semen and the contact of the hormone with the cervix is sometimes enough to begin labor. It is certainly much more enjoyable than an IV, so it's worth a try. Breast stimulation also seems to help.

Relaxation and good breathing

The skills of relaxation and good breathing help prepare you to cope with the stress and pain associated with childbirth. You'll feel much better during labor if you can conserve your energy and keep calm; and if you can relax the muscles under your conscious control, the involuntary muscles of your uterus can work without interference. Knowing that you can breathe calmly and keep your body relaxed at moments of stress gives you the confidence to cope with contractions.

Like any skills, relaxation and good breathing have to be practiced – and that means starting well in advance, so that they become a natural response. However, the uses of relaxation and good breathing are not limited to labor. You and your partner will find many opportunities to use these skills – and not just practice them – during the months of pregnancy itself. The prospect of caring for your new baby is an exciting challenge, but it can also make you anxious, about finances or your freedom of movement, for example, so the ability to relax can be very helpful. If you are having your baby after starting a career, and want to continue working until the last few weeks of your pregnancy, you may let yourself in for a good deal of tension, as well as sheer physical fatigue. Most women know instinctively that they need more rest, and enjoy the slowing down; but if you are working, this need may clash with the demands of the job. Some women regard relaxation simply as a waste of time, and become annoyed and confused when their bodies tell them to slow down. It sometimes takes a conscious effort to let go if you've become hooked on too much stress. Even brief breaks for relaxation during working hours help you cope until you can get proper rest.

By practicing relaxation and good breathing, you'll be doing something for your baby as well as yourself. Babies, before they are born as well as afterward, thrive best in a calm and temperate environment: they need relaxed mothers. You can't eliminate all tension from your life – the right amount is good for you. But you can learn to regulate it, preventing it from causing you undue stress. By practicing the skills of relaxation and breathing, you can make sure that the tension in your life gives you a healthy challenge and doesn't push you beyond your personal limits.

After your baby is born, you'll find the habit of taking relaxation breaks during your busy days and nights will enable you to cope with the demands made on you. The staggering fatigue of the first few weeks, physical and emotional, makes it essential that you know how to care for yourself. To keep your relationship alive as a couple, not just as parents, it is very important to give some special time to each other when, however briefly, you can take some time for relaxation and for giving each other some attention.

If you already have several children, and particularly if you're kept awake at night, try resting while they play. Learn to relax without letting noise and distractions upset your concentration. This is excellent practice for labor, particularly in a hospital, where you're unlikely to find complete peace and tranquility.

Head-to-toe relaxation

You can practice the following routine every day in the same way that you brush your teeth. More subtly, you also need to cultivate the self-awareness that goes with the physical movements. Your aim is not just to learn a technique, but also to deepen your awareness of your body, and of how your mind and body influence each other. For your body reflects your mind – any anxieties or mental tensions, including subconscious ones, are expressed in some form of muscular tension. Your response to the relaxation routine and to the exercises on pages 77–8 will help you discover your particular "map" of muscle tension. This can take time, and you'll find it easier if you do it with a friend or your partner – someone who can read out instructions, help you to see and feel areas of tension and encourage you into a state of mind in which you're willing to relax. If the same person can be with you in labor, so much the better: you'll have the security of being with someone who knows you almost as well as you know yourself. If you're alone, read through all the instructions before you start: you may like to record them on tape to give yourself a running commentary.

Tension needs an outlet, or some form of expression. People often sigh, stretch or yawn instinctively when they feel tense – try singing or dancing next time you feel yourself tightening up. Once you have the knack, you can immediately release the part of your body that needs it, but in the beginning try movement as a prelude to relaxation.

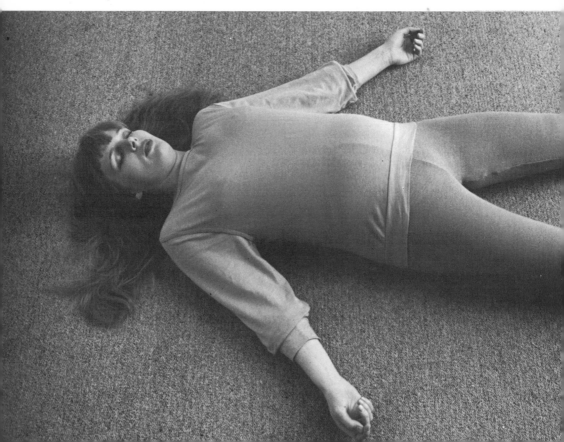

Start by taking a brisk stroll round the garden or living room. Walk as tall as you can, lifting your head, stretching, swinging and shaking your arms. Expand your chest with some deep breaths and sing some long notes. Try pelvic rocking or some belly dancing if the mood strikes you. Stretch your fingers and let them go, so they are loose; shake your wrists. Slap yourself all over with your floppy fingers to liven up your circulation, stopping when you feel deliciously warm all over. If your neck feels tense, do the exercises on pages 42–3 and the self-massage on page 90. After you've moved, warmed and stretched yourself, you can begin the next stage.

Lie on your back on the floor with your legs bent, feet on the floor, hip-width apart. If you're uncomfortable lying on your back, lie on your side (see page 81), adapting the instructions accordingly. Have a selection of cushions nearby to support your head and thighs. At first, it's helpful to practice in a warm room and a calm, quiet atmosphere, considering each part of your body carefully; later on, you'll be able to relax anywhere, in almost any position. After each movement in the sequence, pause and appreciate the comfort you've achieved.

Start at the center of your body – the pelvis. Press it into the floor, slowly flattening your lower back until it feels completely supported and at ease. Think of the rest of your body radiating out from your pelvis.

When you are ready, move up to your shoulders and arms. Press your head and elbows into the floor to lift your chest a little. Pull your shoulder blades together and down, and then flatten and spread them into the floor. Rotate your arms, so your palms face up, and ease your elbows away from your trunk by sliding them along the floor. Stretch your fingers out and apart; hold for a moment and then release them. Repeat if necessary to make sure your fingers are relaxed.

Roll your head gently from side to side; stop in the center. Lower your chin slightly to lengthen the back of your neck and then press your head into the floor – hold this for a moment, and release. Repeat if necessary.

Now concentrate on your face. Do two or three exaggerated smiles, holding each for a second. Drop your lower jaw and move it slowly from side to side. Leaving your mouth slightly open, let your tongue rest low in your mouth, behind your lower teeth. Blink slowly a few times and then leave your eyes closed. Smooth out any frown by lifting your eyebrows once or twice. Feel your face opening out from the center.

Once your eyes are closed, it's easier to shift your concentration to the inside of your body – so work down through your trunk back to your pelvis, adjusting any area that feels tense. Slowly straighten your legs, sliding them down together, and turning out your thighs so your knees roll outward. Gently push your heels away from you and then gently push your toes away. If your feet are stiff or you tend to get cramps, circle your feet instead. You should now feel that your whole body is relaxed.

Calming your mind

When your body is completely relaxed, you'll probably find that your mind has begun to slow down too. This process of calming the mind is essential to maintaining muscle release. If your mind continues to race, sooner or later your body will react and become tense again. The concentration needed to calm your mind also forms part of your preparation for labor, when you must continue to relax your body in spite of internal upheavals and outside distractions.

One way is to use a mantra – by repeating a particular sound, you exclude intrusive thoughts and achieve a state of calm. Another method uses selective imagination: you imagine a calming scene and by putting yourself into it, you exclude ordinary thoughts and worries.

Perhaps the simplest way is to concentrate on your breathing. Focus on the flow of air as it passes into your body, and then sigh it gently out. Be aware of how your body is responding – perhaps you can feel your ribs moving slightly? Don't force your breathing or try to interfere with your natural rhythm.

Whichever method you select, try to enjoy the present without allowing your thoughts to create tension in your body and without exciting your mind by rushing into the future or stirring up the past.

Relaxation ripple

After you've practiced the complete relaxation several times, you can condense the movements into one continuous "ripple" that takes only a moment or two to do. Begin with a pelvic tilt (see pages 14–15); drop your shoulders and lengthen the back of your neck upward; flop your arms, and stretch and flop your hands; close your eyes and drop your lower jaw; spread your thighs and turn out your knees; move your feet about and flop them. Take one or two deep breaths as you flow through the sequence. This is an important skill to practice, as this is the way to welcome and end each contraction.

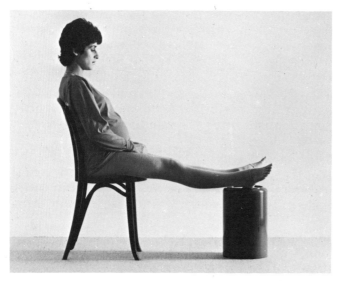

Relaxation in action
Adapt this relaxation ripple to suit your particular needs. You can use it to settle quickly into complete relaxation or whenever you feel yourself tensing up, whether you're lying down, standing or sitting. Choose a "trigger" action, such as dropping your shoulders and lengthening the back of your neck upward on a slow breath out; with practice, you can train yourself so that this trigger sets off a relaxation reaction throughout your body.

Relaxation exercises

Practice these exercises after the complete relaxation sequence. You don't have to do them all at once: just try out each of them and then use whichever you find helpful. Make sure you've read the instructions before you begin. You'll need a partner to practice with, preferably the person who'll be with you in labor. These exercises help to build up trust and understanding between you; secure in that trust, you'll be better able to cope with the stress of labor together.

Fantasy in relaxation

It is normal in pregnancy to experience an increase in dreams and fantasies, both pleasant and unpleasant; talking about these helps you and your partner alleviate your anxieties and share your contentment. It's particularly important to bring hopes and fears about birth into the open, as fears that you've anticipated won't threaten your concentration in labor. By allowing someone to share any fears, however small they may appear, you will find reassurance and the strength to overcome them, and you'll also be able to distinguish any problems that have ready solutions.

After practicing your relaxation, begin to rehearse your labor with your partner or a friend. Imagine how you will feel at the onset and try to imagine all the possible things that might happen, how you'll feel and how you'll cope. Take your time and talk about anything that comes to mind. Your partner should not interrupt, or make comments, but should allow you to wander from idea to idea, until a response is needed. You can both use this technique to help you confront fears about coping with the baby as well.

Improving bodily awareness

This exercise helps you and your partner understand how muscle tension and breathing can be influenced by imagination. When you feel quite at ease, think about the sounds you can hear around you. Don't try to blot them out, but take note of each individual sound and then let it fade into the background. Observe how you are breathing and then give a couple of slow, sighing-out breaths to help yourself release any remaining tension.

Imagine you are lying comfortably in the sunshine. The sun is wonderfully warm on your body, and you have no worries or responsibilities. There's a slight breeze, which is moving the leaves of a large tree. In the distance you can hear the sound of water gently lapping against the shore. Elaborate the scene for yourself or ask your partner to continue for you. After you've enjoyed this scene for a while, observe any changes in your body and breathing.

Imagine now that you are late for an important appointment. It's crucial that you get there, but your car won't start, and there is no other means of transportation. So you decide to run, but your shoes are painful and it's a long way to go. Suddenly you hear a car coming and wave frantically to make it stop, but the car goes straight past you.

Observe the differences in your breathing and body tension during the last scene. Discuss them with your partner, who may have noticed something you were unaware of yourself. You should each experience both scenes.

Touch relaxation

Both this exercise and the next help you to communicate with your partner without words, which is helpful during labor when you want to be confident that your body language is understood. During labor, it's sometimes difficult to express what you need in words, but if your partner can recognize any signs of tension, he'll know how to help you and you'll trust what he does.

This routine helps you to relax toward your partner's touch and helps him to see and feel the difference between tension and relaxation in your body. Although in labor your partner is the one who helps to monitor your tension, and the instructions here are directed at him, it's a good idea for you to help each other in turn, so you both experience being the participant.

After your relaxation routine, touch your partner's body, noticing carefully how each area feels when completely relaxed. Start with her arm: rest your hand on her upper arm, rocking it gently to and fro. Now lift it a little and let it fall back; notice if there's any tightening. Try not to make any sudden or jerking movements that might disturb your partner's concentration as you work round her body, but observe when she tightens up or pulls away from you so you can discuss it later. When you touch her head, don't lift it up, but just rock it gently from side to side – this is the part of the body that it's most difficult to trust someone else to move.

Ask your partner to tense her shoulders as tightly as she can. Sit between her legs as she relaxes back against a wall, and rest your hands on her shoulders, asking her to release them under your hands. Do this a few times, until your partner relaxes instinctively at your touch, dropping her shoulders under the warmth and weight of your hands. Repeat with other areas that tend to tense up – arms, hands or thighs – so your partner becomes used to relaxing in response to your touch.

Trust in movement

This exercise helps to build up trust by allowing your partner to take complete responsibility for you, and so may be difficult for people who find it hard to be passive. You should both take turns at it; the instructions here are for the woman.

Ask your partner to sit down and close his eyes. Neither of you should now speak. After a pause, stand your partner up, holding his arm firmly. Lead him round the room, being careful not to let him trip or bump into anything. Now sit him down again and give him a variety of objects to touch and hold. Don't do anything too startling or the trust will be broken. Take your partner outside and let him feel the sun or wind on his face. If there's an open space, walk and then run slowly with him. Be very gentle as you let him experience as many different sensations as possible in your care. After you've finished, discuss how the exercise felt for each of you.

You can also try mirroring each other's movements. Stand up facing each other and move your arms, legs, head or trunk slowly and rhythmically, while your partner tries to follow your movements in silence. Look at each other closely as you do this, so that you become accustomed to tuning in to each other without communicating with words.

Good breathing

This goes hand in hand with your relaxation skills. Breathing and relaxation together give you dual awareness of body tensions, which in turn positively influences your state of mind, for your breathing is affected by the way you are feeling, and by the same token the way you feel can be influenced by the way you breathe. "Good" breathing is breathing that's appropriate to your needs and doesn't make you tense up or feel out of control. You already know how you breathe when you're completely relaxed (see page 76); try the second exercise on page 77 to see how your breathing alters when you are happy, upset or excited. By practicing the whole range of deep to shallow breathing, you can experience the effect that different levels have on your mind and body, while you consciously keep your body relaxed.

Although it's important not to force yourself to breathe unnaturally, especially during contractions, it's helpful to discover your range and develop the confidence to keep your whole body relaxed no matter what kind of breathing you do. You'll develop the skill to relax if you're tense or panicky by using the calming deep breathing and to remain at ease if you feel the need to breathe more lightly.

Deep breathing

Sit down comfortably, with your back to your partner. Make sure that your shoulders are down and your face and hands are relaxed. Ask your partner to place his hands firmly just above your waistline. Try to make his hands move as you breathe *in* through your nose and gently *out* through your mouth. Concentrate on sighing your breath *out* gently and slowly; the *in* breath will follow naturally. Don't talk to your partner – he should wait, keeping his hands still, until your breathing settles into a steady rhythm. This is the calming pattern to be used whenever you feel the need, and always at the beginning and end of each contraction (see pages 95–6).

If you find it hard to breathe deeply or feel there isn't room, don't try to force yourself. Instead ask your partner to move his hands up a little and try the exercise again. As you learn to relax, your breathing will automatically become deeper.

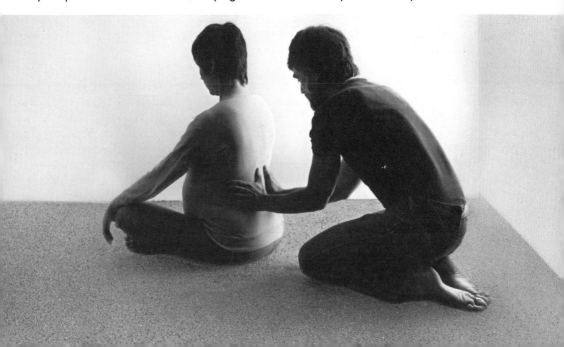

Light breathing
Ask your partner to move his hands up to your shoulder blades. Begin to breathe more lightly, keeping your mouth open, so you breathe *in* and *out* through slightly parted lips. Keep your tongue low to prevent your mouth getting too dry. As you relax into this lighter, faster rhythm, you'll feel your body vibrate slightly, like an echo. If you need to take a deep breath occasionally, that's all right. You'll probably find this breathing useful in labor for the peaks of the more difficult contractions: it will come naturally in labor.

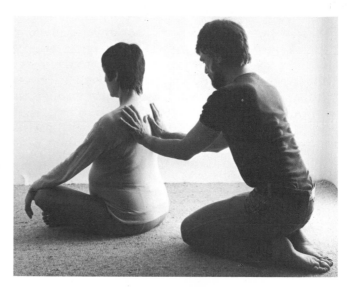

Feather-light breathing
This is the lightest breathing. For your partner to check this, he should rest his hands on top of your shoulders, his middle fingers on your collar bone – he will only feel a slight vibration as you breathe.
   Keeping your mouth slightly open, breathe as lightly as you can, imagining that you're lifting a feather off your palm and letting it settle again. If you find this makes you gasp, relax your throat and take a deeper breath when you want to. This pattern shows you how lightly it's possible to breathe during a contraction without becoming breathless.

When you feel confident, ask your partner to move his hands from position to position and, without talking, to wait for you to adapt your breathing. When he feels each rhythm is comfortably established, he can move to another position. This is good practice for labor when you have to respond to contractions, which are not under your control. Remember that contractions don't last much longer than a minute, and that you can rest between them.
   Another essential part of preparing for labor is to practice breathing "into" pain. You've already used breathing to help you cope with the stretch created by some of the key positions (see page 25). Now combine your skills by trying out the different breathing levels as you practice the key positions – find out which helps you cope with the discomfort most effectively.

Getting comfortable

You may find it increasingly difficult to get comfortable as your pregnancy progresses. Look at the suggestions here and adapt them to suit yourself. Just remember to keep your body as symmetrical as possible, as this will help you to remain even and balanced. If you develop any tension spots, adjusting your position will help you to sort them out: they'll get worse if you ignore them.

below Lying on your back is an excellent position in which to relax, as the whole body is well supported. However, there is good evidence to suggest that lying on your back for long periods is not a good idea in late pregnancy, and you will probably find it uncomfortable in the last weeks. This is because the weight of the uterus presses down on the main veins and arteries that run up your back, making you feel faint, breathless or slightly nauseous. Your lungs can't function as well when you lie on your back, either. This is why it's not a good position for labor. So, if you don't find lying on your back a comfortable position, try propping yourself up with some cushions.

below Lying on your side may make you more comfortable in late pregnancy. Try bending the top leg and placing one, two or even three cushions or pillows under the top thigh. Don't have too many pillows under your head, as this makes your spine bow. You may find it more comfortable to have your arm bent back behind you. Don't tighten or hunch your shoulders up – pull them down away from your ears.

Touching, stroking and holding are the most direct ways of communicating with those you love. Within the family, touch and massage not only provide an ideal opportunity to get closer to each other, but are the most immediate and effective ways of giving comfort, whether to a crying baby, a tired and fretful child or an over-stressed partner.

The kind of massage suggested below is at everybody's fingertips; indeed, it's a form of talking with your hands – stroking and comfort touching rather than a professional massage. The important thing is wanting to give to the person you are touching. This means experimenting together and giving feedback and suggestions: if a stroke doesn't feel right, show your partner how you want it done; if it feels good, do it again. For the couple, this kind of massage enlarges the range of direct communication, with the added bonus that during labor it's likely to be very helpful.

During labor some part of your body may feel uncomfortable, whether from cramps, tension or shivering, and you'll want massage, stroking or just firm holding to help you feel better. This desire to be held is a universal need, for comfort and pleasure. In labor it varies from woman to woman and can also come and go within one labor; but everyone prefers being touched by someone they already know and trust. If you've been exploring massage as a way of communicating with your partner, it will seem natural and easy during labor. Try the touch relaxation exercise on page 78 to help you become more aware of each other's patterns of body tension.

Preparation
Touch is an instant communication of feeling, so to enable someone else to relax you must relax yourself first. If you are tense, try to unwind before you begin: a relaxation ripple (see page 76) may help, as may simply shaking your hands out. Always make sure your partner is warm and comfortable before beginning. If he or she is lying down, make sure it's on a firm surface and that there are plenty of cushions. It's also important that you are comfortable and that you don't have to lean at an awkward angle to reach your partner.

If you just want to massage or stroke your partner's back or shoulders, you can do it quite satisfactorily through clothes: it's always better to release tension before it builds up into pain, and even a few minutes of massage help. However, when you decide to practice massage for labor it's better to do it on bare skin, as this allows you to feel how the muscles react. Start each movement with gentle pressure, increasing it if your partner asks you to, and repeat each as often as you like. Wash your hands to feel cool and fresh and use talcum powder, moisturizer or massage oil on bare skin so that the skin doesn't get "burned". Finally, bear in mind that every skill needs practice, so be patient and loving with each other while you are learning.

If you want to work through the whole massage, allow at least half an hour and make sure you won't be interrupted. However, there's no need to follow the sequence: spend time on the parts of the body that feel tense and improvise your strokes as you build up your expertise and your knowledge of your partner's preferences and needs.

Face and head

below This is excellent for headaches, or to release tension in the scalp. Have your partner lie propped up against your chest. Gently close her eyelids with your fingertips, resting them there until she's lost the urge to open her eyes. Now mold your hands round her head and rock her head slowly from side to side to make sure her neck is relaxed. With gentle pressure, squeeze her head between your hands. Pause for a few seconds, then slowly lift your hands away.

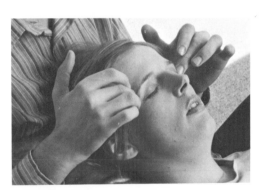

left Place your fingertips between your partner's eyebrows. Press gently with your middle fingers as you smooth out any frown, and stroke outward over each eyebrow until you feel the slight hollow at each temple. Press down gently and lift your fingers off.

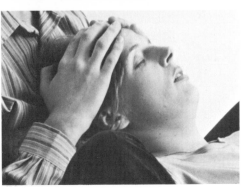

left Rest your fingers on your partner's forehead so they just touch in the middle. Stroke outward, smoothing out the skin, and gently brush your fingers off her head.

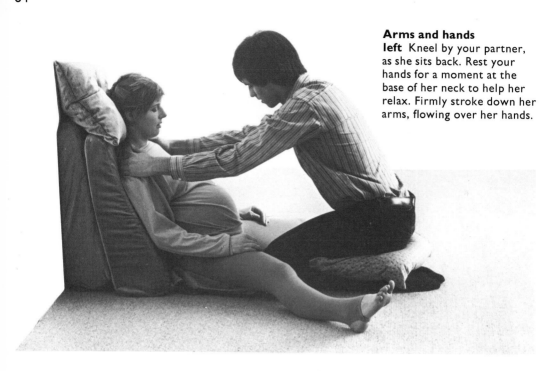

Arms and hands

left Kneel by your partner, as she sits back. Rest your hands for a moment at the base of her neck to help her relax. Firmly stroke down her arms, flowing over her hands.

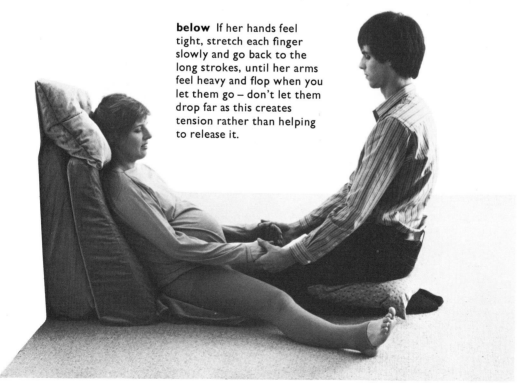

below If her hands feel tight, stretch each finger slowly and go back to the long strokes, until her arms feel heavy and flop when you let them go – don't let them drop far as this creates tension rather than helping to release it.

Neck, shoulders and back
right Have your partner sit
the wrong way round on a
chair, leaning forward onto a
cushion. This position is good
for early labor as leaning
forward takes the weight of
the baby off the lower back.
The neck is particularly
sensitive, so rest your hands
on the skin before you begin.
Mold your hands over your
partner's shoulders and
squeeze upward, bringing
your thumbs gently up to
meet your fingers.

right Place your hands on
either side of your partner's
spine, at the base. Sweep up
the spine in one flowing
movement, pressing firmly
with the heels of your hands.
Take the stroke up to the
shoulders. You can also
practice this stroke and the
next one with your partner
lying on her side.

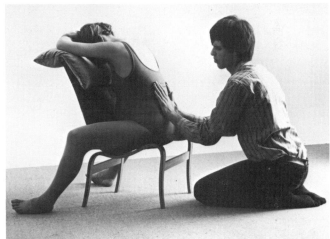

right Make sure your
partner's head is tipped
slightly forward. Using the
heel of one hand, stroke
slowly and firmly up the
length of the spine, ending at
the base of the skull.

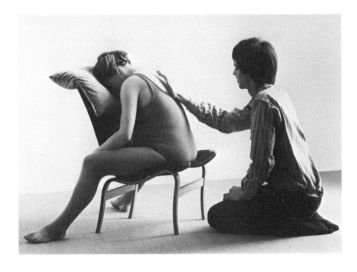

**Lower back and thighs
right** Massage for low back
pain in labor is best done by
using firm pressure. To
practice this, ask your
partner to lie on her side with
her back straight, her upper
leg resting on a pillow. Using
the widest part of your palm,
place your hand between her
buttocks, pressing firmly on
the tip of the coccyx. Slowly
and firmly move the flesh over
the bone, using a circular
motion. Your partner can also
rock her pelvis against the
pressure of your hand.

below This is also a good
position for thigh massage.
Mold your hands round the
back of your partner's thighs
and firmly stroke upward from
knee level, finishing at the
buttocks. In labor, you can
also knead the buttocks to
help relieve cramps.

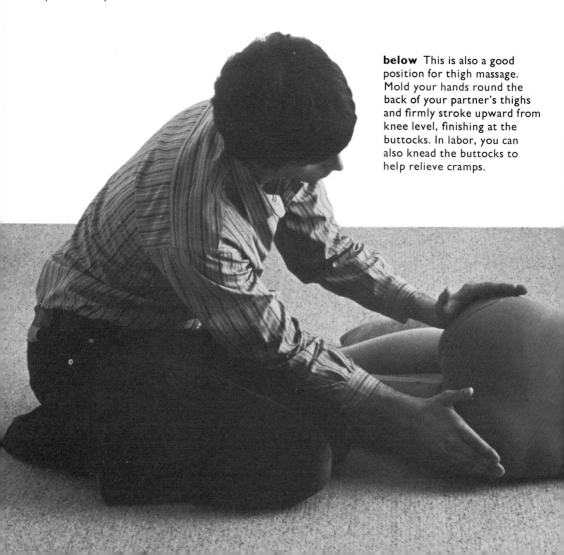

Feet
above and left Ask your partner to sit so she's fully supported; rest one of her legs along yours, so you can sit with a straight back, and put a cushion under her foot. Take her foot firmly in your hands and press your thumbs along the sole and out to the edges of her foot. Pressing firmly helps to make this less ticklish. Start at the heel and work your way up to the toes. When you've finished, gently stretch out each toe. Repeat with the other foot.

Self-massage

Every day throughout pregnancy your body gradually changes shape – you can see your breasts and your abdomen swelling. Gentle self-massage not only keeps your skin supple, if you use a moisturizer, but also allows you to appreciate your wonderful shape through touch. Try closing your eyes – your tactile awareness will increase. Give yourself time to enjoy this exploration of the senses – it's all part of preparing yourself for childbirth.

Self-massage feels good and helps to prevent tension developing into pain. If one part of your body is taking too much strain it upsets your overall harmony.

Face and head

left Close your eyes while massaging your face and head, if this helps you to relax. Place your fingertips on either side of your nose, just under your eyes. Very lightly at first, smooth outward under your eyes. Finish at the slight hollow at your temples: press gently and lift your fingers off. Repeat, starting each stroke slightly lower down your face, but always ending at the same point. Continue until you reach the jaw line, feeling that you are opening out your face.

right This stroke and the next two in the sequence are especially good for relieving tension. Spread your fingers apart a little and, starting just above your eyebrows, stroke up your forehead with your fingertips to the hairline, smoothing out any furrows. With your fingers at your hairline, rock your scalp forward and back a few times.

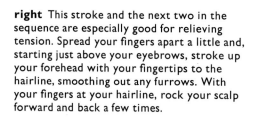

above With the middle finger of each hand, follow the line of each eyebrow from the middle outward. When you reach your temples, circle slowly round with both fingertips, using as much pressure as is effective and comfortable.

above Spread your fingers out. Slide them up over each side of your scalp, starting above and behind your ears, until they meet at the top of your head. Lift your hands away from your head, allowing your hair to slip between your fingers.

Body massage

A good time to massage your abdomen, hips, thighs and breasts is after you shower or bathe or when you're getting dressed. Start with your lower abdomen, making slow, gentle, circular strokes with both hands. Then, if you want, try some firmer strokes, going up and over the bulge: imagine that you are lifting the baby back into the pelvis. End the strokes at the top of the bulge and come round and back to the side again. This is particularly comforting toward the end of pregnancy. Start again at the sides, using the same stroke, but continue up and round your breasts.

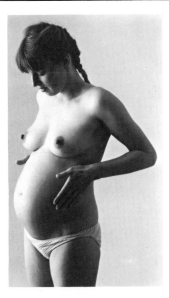

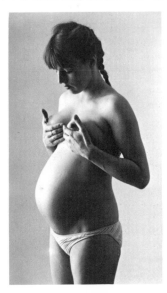

Neck

right Turn your head to the left. Mold your right hand over the left side of your neck and firmly sweep over the back of your neck and off to the front. Repeat on the other side, looking to the right.

Shoulders

left Begin by circling your shoulders backward, as on page 45. Pause and focus on your breathing, allowing your shoulders to relax down a little more with each slow breath out. Mold your left hand over your right shoulder, holding the flesh firmly and circle your shoulder backward again. Increase the pressure of your hand as feels comfortable. Repeat on the other side.

Abdomen

right This is particularly good in early labor, to help you relax. Imagine you are stroking the baby's head as you very lightly brush your fingertips across the underside of your abdomen, first with one hand, then the other.

Ankles and feet

left Sit on a chair, a stool or on the floor. Bend one leg across the other, resting your ankle over the opposite knee and letting your foot hang freely. Clasp your foot with both hands and circle it round a few times to relax the ankle. With your thumbs, massage the sole from heel to toe, and back again. When you've finished, stretch out each toe, circling the big one; if your toes feel stiff, try the exercises on page 55. Repeat with the other foot.

For the mother and baby, labor is the beginning of the process of separation. They have appeared as one being, until contractions start, although the mother knows the baby is already an individual. Labor is the bridge between the union of pregnancy and the beginning of life as two separate people: the mother needs it as much as the baby, to help her adjust from pregnancy to motherhood.

_____ Planning your labor _____

What kind of labor and birth experience do you want? Giving birth can be an intensely intimate experience, physically and emotionally powerful for both partners, or it can be reduced to an impersonal routine of technical procedures. Sadly, the tendency is to deny choice to women and their partners, to whittle away their control. The routine use of drugs, fetal monitoring, episiotomies, and so forth, in sterile, impersonal surroundings has tended to alienate the couple from the birth experience. It has made women passive and dependent, so that labor becomes psychologically and physically less satisfactory for the woman and her partner.

Nevertheless, you can take responsibility for the kind of treatment you receive. By learning the skills presented in this book – and going to childbirth classes as well – you are preparing yourself for a more satisfying birth experience. But it isn't just a question of acquiring new skills and self-confidence. If you're to benefit from them, you'll have to make sure that the people who care for you during your labor are sympathetic to your approach, which means planning as much as possible in advance.

Read through this chapter and look at the further reading list: once you know what kind of birth you're aiming at, you can discuss it with your medical team. If you want a home birth, find out what arrangements you have to make; even if you're planning to be at home it's worth talking about procedures with your back-up hospital. Ask your doctor or midwife what their routine is; if you want something different, discuss it and try to find an approach that's safe for you and the baby and also feels right for you. The agreement of any requests that are not standard for your hospital can be written on your hospital notes to avoid arguments when you're in labor. Remember that it's not a black-and-white choice between a "mechanized" and a "natural" birth – there are many shades of variety in between – so don't give up if you encounter opposition to some of your requests, but try to be flexible and find compromises. The checklist below is intended as a guide to the points to raise: above all, don't be afraid to ask.

- Make sure you can be upright and mobile for as long as you feel comfortable.
- Ask if your partner can be with you throughout labor, even if you need a Caesarean delivery. If you want another helper with you for support in the second stage (see pages 103–4), find out if that's possible.
- Visit the labor room and find out if you'll have to move into a different room for delivery. Look carefully at the furniture and plan how to adapt it to give you a choice of positions (see pages 98–105) during labor. Don't take anything for granted; you may need to bring even the simplest things to make yourself comfortable, from extra cushions to a stool.

- Find out what to expect if you need medical intervention. Which drugs are usually available? Which, if any, may be given at your hospital and what are their possible effects on you and your baby? Which anesthetics are likely to make you feel nauseated, and what alternatives are there? Will you always be examined internally to assess how far your cervix has dilated, and consulted, *before* being given drugs? If you need an IV, is it possible to have a portable one? If you have an epidural (an anesthetic injected into the epidural space of one of the lower vertebrae), can you deliver in an upright position, supported on both sides? Can you remain awake if you need a Caesarean delivery? If your labor doesn't go according to plan, there's no need to feel like a failure or to give up your active involvement – be ready to adapt.
- When will labor be induced.and what methods will be used?
- Is fetal monitoring routine throughout labor (either externally on your abdomen or through a device clipped to your baby's head), or is it used only for high-risk patients? Discuss with the medical staff how monitoring may affect your mobility.
- Discuss the delivery. Find out which positions your midwife or doctor is prepared to use. Is there a birth chair or bed in your hospital? If you want to squat or kneel, can you do this on the floor or bed? If you can't deliver in this position, can you at least be upright for pushing at the beginning of second-stage labor? Is there a midwife or nurse happy to help support you in the positions on pages 103–4? Find out whether your baby can be delivered onto your abdomen and how soon the umbilical cord will be cut. Can you and your partner be left alone with the baby after the birth? Ask about the hospital's attitude toward breastfeeding. Discuss whether your baby can be with you at all times.

If you have any problems, make an appointment to see your most senior medical adviser with your partner, so you can try to find a satisfactory solution. Make sure your partner knows what you want and can help you deal with all the stages of labor. Well prepared, you can avoid sudden surprises or needless anxiety and concentrate on the labor – enough of a surprise in itself.

What happens in labor

One day your labor will start quite mysteriously and, once begun, nothing that you do can stop its progress. Everyone has fears, especially about a first baby. For most women, pregnant with their first child, thinking about labor means wondering about contractions: every book gives a different description of how they feel and other women are either maddeningly vague or gruesomely vivid in their evocation of these mysterious waves of energy.

You have to "give" birth and as the contractions grow steadily stronger you and the baby are taken over by the tremendous force of energy flowing between you. If you're able, you'll gradually abandon yourself to the sensations flowing through your body – as you do during intense love-making – while being irresistibly drawn toward the inevitable climax of the birth itself.

During labor the baby is embraced and massaged by each contraction. This seems to be a positive experience, which also plays a part in preparing the baby's system for life outside. Birth is not necessarily painful for the mother or the baby. Almost all women feel some pain during labor; but most remember the satisfaction that comes from accepting the kind of pain that is part of pleasure. Feeling part of the flow of life itself gives women inspiration in labor – heightening their self-awareness and drawing out the capacity to give, which they will perfect as mothers.

The first stage of labor is said to have begun when strong contractions come regularly; it progresses as these uterine waves become gradually stronger and more frequent. Powerful and involuntary contractions start at the top of the uterus, where they are strongest, and ripple down, spreading out over the whole uterus as they pull up the lower section (or segment) and dilate the cervix. The upper part of the uterus pushes down on the baby, whose head in turn presses down on the cervix, helping it to dilate. Between these rhythmic waves of muscle activity, the uterus doesn't completely relax but retains each small retraction so that the cervix is thinned, pulled and stretched up round the baby's head with gathering speed until the birth canal is completely open.

There's often a phase just before the end of the first stage when many women feel they can't cope any longer: this is known as transition. The loss of confidence is clearly linked with both physical and emotional fatigue, for the contractions you are coping with are intense and sometimes have two peaks instead of one. Physical symptoms, such as nausea or trembling, may worsen or develop. Nothing helps and your desperation is expressed by loss of confidence in yourself or sudden anger or tears. Not everyone experiences signs of transition, so don't get too worried. However, if you do have a difficult transition, don't be afraid to ask for extra holding and massage, or for your partner to keep a tactful distance – whatever you prefer. Try shifting from side to side and see if that helps; try getting more upright as well. Remember that the cervix dilates faster in the second half of the first stage, so you're probably almost fully dilated.

In the second stage of labor, your body is ready to allow your baby to be born. Now, at last, you can work actively with your body. Whereas in the first stage you had to remain as relaxed as possible while your uterus did its work, you can now use your diaphragm and abdominal muscles to help the downward thrust of the uterine contractions. These contractions are not necessarily painful, except for the unbelievable feeling of stretching wider and wider. As the baby's head drops down onto the pelvic floor, the urge to push becomes overwhelming; and as the second stage builds up to its climax, you feel a great surge of power and pleasure in your body – similar to an orgasm in that there's no holding back – which culminates in the birth.

The third stage of labor is the delivery of the placenta. This happens quite quickly after the birth. The baby should be safely in your arms and the umbilical cord may already have been cut by the time this happens. If you can, have a look at this remarkable organ that has sustained your baby for so long.

The fourth stage is getting to know your baby and becoming a family – this is quite as strenuous as labor itself and takes a good deal longer!

Breathing awareness

Whether you have been regularly practicing relaxation and breathing or you've picked up this book on the way to your last antenatal checkup, there's no need to worry about breathing during labor. Breathing is an involuntary process: your body adjusts to the demand, whatever the task. Have you ever thought of taking lessons in breathing for running up stairs, or making love?

If you've looked at books with complicated breathing rules and wondered how on earth you can remember them all, the answer is simple – you probably won't. When labor gets difficult, you'll fall back on whatever comes naturally, so instead of learning other people's breathing rules, find out what's most comfortable and feels best for you and then allow your body to take over, bearing in mind the guidelines below. The only occasion when special breathing is helpful is if you need to stop yourself pushing (see page 96).

However, nobody denies that there's pain in childbirth, so the problem of how to cope with it remains. Distraction with methods of complicated breathing patterns is taught to many women preparing for childbirth. In general, though, distraction is successful for only a limited time: eventually the woman in labor has to accept the messages coming from her body and adjust accordingly. Also, attempting too much control during contractions encourages tension to build up. The guidelines in this book stem from the Kitzinger "associative" approach, which suggests focusing on sensations and flowing with them, whereas methods based on the Lamaze theory rely on teaching pregnant women a "dissociative" coping style, which distracts the woman from pain. Turn to page 126 for further reading and decide which approach appeals to you naturally: then build on that to help yourself during labor.

Whichever method you choose, it's important to practice observing and interpreting your body's signals: try the exercises on pages 77–8 to build up your body awareness. With faith in yourself, you can manage any physically or emotionally demanding event and, secure in your capacity to cope with pain, you can relax when labor starts, trusting in the natural process and letting go at the moment of birth.

Practical guidelines for the first stage

Breathing
- Never hold your breath. Both you and your baby need as much oxygen as possible during labor.
- Never breathe out too hard, as this can lead to hyperventilation – an imbalance of oxygen and carbon dioxide, which is dangerous for mother and baby if it continues too long. If you begin to feel faint or have tingling in your fingers, cup one or both hands over your mouth and breathe in and out into your hands until you feel better. Ask for guidance if it persists. Your partner should listen for heavy breathing out.
- At the beginning of each contraction, take a few slow, calming breaths in, sighing out gently (see page 79). Make these breaths the signal to do a relaxation ripple (see page 76), focusing your concentration on whatever your body is telling you it needs.

- As the wave of the contraction builds up, keep your breathing regular, slow and rhythmic while you try to keep your whole body as relaxed as possible. You may find that you naturally use the light or feather-light breathing on page 80 for part of some contractions.
- As the wave starts to fade away, do a few more slow, calming breaths and another relaxation ripple.
- Between contractions, allow your breathing to regulate itself. You need adjust it consciously only if you're gasping or unable to relax, in which case continue the calming breathing until you feel better. Between contractions, try to keep as calm as possible, saving your energy whenever you can. Your partner can help by protecting you from disturbance, particularly during contractions, allowing you to reach a level of concentrated awareness, which helps you counter the pain naturally and induces a sense of well-being.

Breathing for uneven dilation of the cervix
If your cervix dilates unevenly, you may feel you want to start pushing before you are physically ready to: the birth canal is not completely open, so you'll be told not to push. Try the position opposite to help you with this, with the following breathing. As the contraction begins take a few calming breaths, doing your relaxation ripple (see page 76). When the urge to push becomes too strong to ignore, say "huff, huff – blow", with a short, light breath in and out as you say each "huff" and a longer breath out on the "blow". This longer breath out helps to prevent you bearing down; repeat your usual routine for the end of contractions as the urge to push fades.

Sounds in labor
Just as everyone can breathe, so everyone can sing. Whatever others may think of your musical abilities, your baby, when born, will love the sound of you singing. It's known that babies can hear in the uterus, so your baby knows the sound of your voice; perhaps you already talk and sing to your baby. When you are in labor, try to sing your way through a contraction – as you sing, you open your chest and relax your mouth and throat. You don't have to sing at top volume, but if you and your partner sing together, it will help your concentration, regulate your breathing and soothe you and your baby.

Some women are worried about making noises that might sound too primitive; but if these sounds help you, they shouldn't be suppressed or ignored. As you get nearer to the second stage, you may hear yourself making the most surprising sounds. Moans, shouts, gutteral groans, let them come, allowing them to relax your·mouth and throat and generally reduce tension.

Movement
During pregnancy, practice getting into the positions on pages 98–105 with your partner, so you know which are comfortable and can move easily from one to another. It's important to discuss this with your medical team: the onus is usually on you to negotiate for freedom of movement. These are not the only positions –

improvise and adapt to find others that suit you, preferably keeping your trunk upright or leaning forward. You can use any of the first-stage positions during the second stage, and vice versa; you can also adapt positions to be used on the bed or the floor depending on your circumstances. In any position, rocking your pelvis helps your baby's head rotate into a more favorable position. This rhythmic rocking is a great help toward the end of the first stage – so practice rocking and good breathing together.

If you're finding the contractions difficult to deal with, try changing position before asking for drugs. Remember to relax completely between contractions, in whatever position feels best. Massage may also help (see pages 82–7). If you opt for an epidural and you have to lie on your side, ask your partner to massage the side you're lying on to help prevent stiffness and try to change sides as often as possible. Support yourself with plenty of pillows and cushions to make yourself comfortable if you're on a hard bed.

Your position and first-stage labor

A woman who stays upright and moves about during the first stage of labor feels more comfortable. Being fairly upright in labor makes your contractions stronger and so more efficient as gravity helps your uterus to bear down: this means that the baby's head presses down more effectively and so helps your cervix to dilate faster, speeding up labor. Moving around helps you to feel actively involved in your labor – and so you tend to feel less pain. Being upright or leaning forward also has the advantage that you're not constricting your circulation – if you lie on your back your uterus presses down on the large blood vessels running down your back. Don't expect labor to be easy or pain-free, but if you think of yourself as an upright, mobile person who happens to be in labor, it will help. If you do have to lie down, try to lie on your side not your back, and don't worry – this doesn't prevent you from having a normal labor.

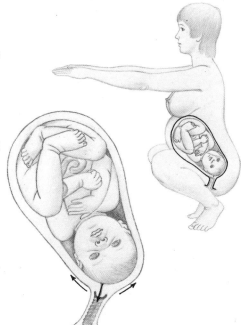

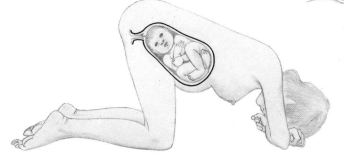

left This position helps if you need to stop pushing in transition. It's harder to push if your bottom is raised like this, as gravity is working against you. The angle of the uterus to the vagina is at its most acute, which also helps to slow down labor.

First-stage positions
left As you walk about at
the start of labor, you may
like to lean forward and rest
against your partner during
contractions. You can also
lean like this onto a wall, but
if your partner is there, you
have the advantage that he can
rub your back.

right If you want to kneel down, you may feel more comfortable if you lean forward onto a chair, resting your arms and head on a cushion. You can also kneel upright or half-kneel with one foot flat on the floor. You may like a cushion under your knees if you're not on a carpet. Between contractions rest to one side and massage your knees, if necessary.

left If you find being upright tiring, kneeling on all fours is reassuring and comfortable. It allows you to rock your pelvis freely and keep the weight of the baby off your lower back, helping to prevent backache. This is also a good position to try if you have difficulties in transition. Sit back on your heels or to one side between contractions.

below If you want to sit down, try sitting the wrong way round on a chair. Lean on a cushion or pillow and allow your shoulders to drop. Make sure your feet are firmly on the floor and that the chair doesn't dig into your legs. Your partner can massage your back easily as you rest like this (see pages 85–6).

above If you want to squat, try leaning forward onto your hands for balance. Rock your weight between your hands and feet. Between contractions, shake or massage your arms if they're getting tense.

right Instead of leaning onto the chair, you may prefer to lean onto your partner, as he kneels in front of you.

Late first-stage positions

By the time you're nearing second stage, your contractions will be more frequent and you may have some of the signs of transition (see page 94). See pages 96–7 for advice on breathing and position for uneven dilation of the cervix.

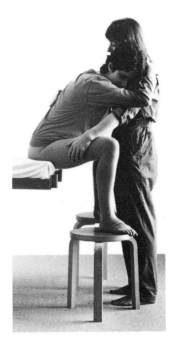

above Try leaning forward onto a pile of cushions or pillows, kneeling with your legs wide apart. The more upright you can be, the better.

right A partner can support and massage you if you sit on the edge of the bed. Rest your feet on two stools if you're on a high hospital bed.

below If you're squatting on a hospital bed, you can use the rails at the end for support. You'll probably feel safer with some support from a partner, as hospital beds are often high and narrow.

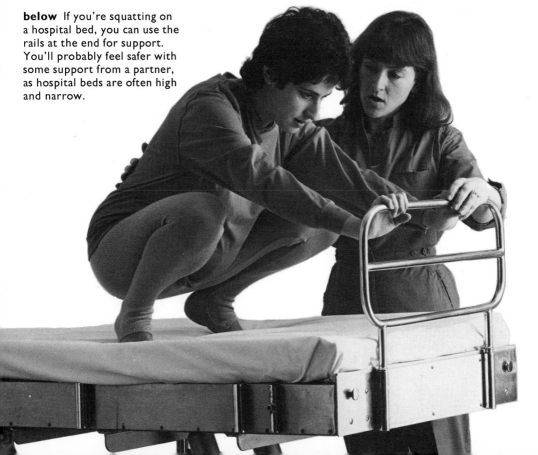

Practical guidelines for the second stage

When you reach the second stage, you'll want to stop moving and take up a comfortable position for delivery. Several of the positions shown here need two helpers – if you can't have an extra friend with you, the midwife or a nurse should be able to help support you. Always take the advice of your midwife or doctor on how fast the delivery should progress, and adjust your position accordingly.

Your position and second-stage labor
If you lie on your back, you literally have to push the baby uphill. If you're upright, your abdominal muscles and diaphragm are more efficient as you bear down and gravity helps to ease your baby's journey. It's easier for the baby's head to pass through the lower opening of the pelvis and it's possible for the pelvic bones to open wider. You're less likely to tear, or need an episiotomy, as the baby's head presses down more evenly and gently through the vaginal outlet. If you do have to lie down, your baby will be born safely, but you'll have to work harder.

Pushing

As each contraction starts, remember to take one or two calming breaths and do a relaxation ripple (see page 76). You'll probably find that you breathe lightly (see page 80) as the contraction builds up, holding your breath instinctively as the urge to push becomes overwhelming, which may happen several times during one contraction, as second-stage contractions last between one and one and a half minutes. As you push, focus on your pelvic floor. Tell these muscles to relax, picturing the baby's head stretching your body and letting yourself go completely. Let your mouth stay open and perhaps talk or sing your baby out of your body. There seems to be an unconscious link between the mouth and vagina, so anything that helps your mouth relax is to be encouraged. Try to keep your face as soft as possible, asking your partner to remind you of these guidelines by whispering as he holds you in his arms; together you can breathe your baby out.

You should not be hurried during the pushing stage: take your time and enjoy the full satisfaction of this amazing feeling. Listen to your midwife or doctor so that you can regulate your pushing efforts sensitively. Rest completely between contractions to gather your strength, sucking on an ice cube or having your face sponged with cool water. Just before the baby's head is delivered the midwife may ask you to stop pushing, allowing the uterus to work alone. Just pant gently as the head oozes slowly out of your vagina, with no extra pressure from your diaphragm or abdominal muscles. Once the head is born, reach down to touch your baby as the rest of the body slithers out, like a waterfall of arms and legs tumbling out of your body; when your baby is delivered on your abdomen, you can cuddle her at last, as she opens her eyes for the first time to look around her.

Second-stage positions

When you're squatting, your pelvis can open to its widest, so you won't have to push so hard. You also have more sensitive awareness of your pelvic floor, so you can relax it more easily (see page 13). You can squat with support on both sides, either on the bed or on the floor. In this supported position you can confidently let go, so that your pelvic floor relaxes completely.

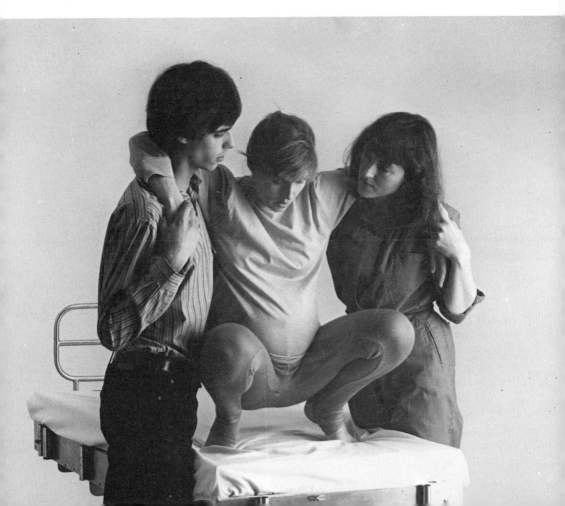

above Your partner can stand behind you, supporting your weight by holding you under your armpits, so that you can let go. You can either hold his hands (left) or clasp your arms up round his neck (right). Your partner should pay particular attention to keeping his back straight, bending his knees if necessary, depending on his height. It's especially important to practice this beforehand and to remember the rules of lifting on page 22.

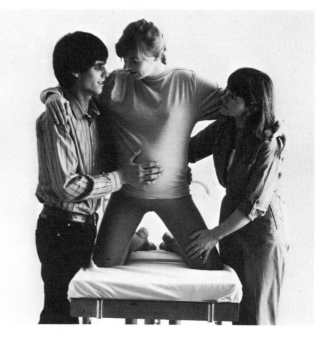

right Kneeling is also a good position for pushing. If you have two helpers you'll feel much safer.

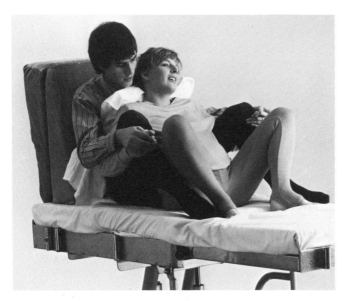

If you prefer to sit back, prop yourself upright on a pile of pillows or cushions and do a pelvic tilt (see pages 14–15), letting your head relax forward, so you're in a banana shape. Most hospitals are happy to deliver in this position. It's more comforting if your partner can sit behind you and support you.

Aids to bring to the hospital

Hospitals usually give out lists of things to bring with you when you go in for labor. Here are a few that they may not have suggested.

- Vaseline or lip salve to prevent your lips getting dry.
- Hard candies or honey to give you energy.
- A small make-up sponge, kept in a thermos of iced water, to suck between contractions, and a thermos filled with an iced drink.
- Warm woolly socks in case you're suddenly cold at the end of the first stage or after the birth.
- Something special: a photo or small picture that you particularly love.
- Food for your partner: if you have a long labor he will get hungry and you may not want him to go away to eat. Take something extra for you too – you'll be ravenous after the birth, and if it's the middle of the night there may not be any food available.
- A cassette recorder to help you relax in the first stage.
- A book or game for you and your partner. If you have a very long labor and an epidural you may need them.
- Lotion, oil or talcum powder for massage.
- One frozen and one heated picnic pack, wrapped in foil, for backache: a hot or cold compress against your lower back may be comforting.
- Coins for the phone.
- Your usual toilet things.
- Front-opening nighties and nursing bras.
- This book, so you can resume exercising soon after the birth.
- Ear plugs, so you can get some sleep on a noisy floor or during the day. Wax ones are the best.
- Any "props" that you've discovered you need, such as extra pillows.

When the excitement and emotion of the birth have begun to fade, you'll lift your gaze from your baby to take a look at yourself. You may get quite a shock. Last time you looked at your body, you had the majesty of a ship in full sail. Now you've lost that – your baby is in the bed beside you, but your body may seem unrecognizable, and the sight of a large and flabby abdomen can be surprising and upsetting. A few lucky people seem to deflate like balloons, but most don't, although everyone loses extra fluid during the first week.

After the birth everything seems to conspire to make you feel anything but back to normal. Whatever kind of labor and delivery you've had, the realities of caring 24 hours a day for a tiny baby are immediately upon you. But as the fog of new sensations and feelings subsides to a gentle haze, you may begin to think about yourself and your body.

Immediately after the birth, your body starts to readjust to its normal rhythms. It can take at least three months to complete this process, and longer if you are breastfeeding, so don't expect too much of yourself. You need an abundance of care; your baby will thrive if you feel contented. Begin exercises when you feel you want to, never force yourself and always enjoy what you are doing – then you'll find time to do more! There are two stages of the postnatal program: the first to be done in the week after delivery, the second covering the remainder of the first three months. Be gentle with yourself but persistent, listening carefully to what your body tells you it needs. Looking after a new baby is in itself a very demanding activity, but you'll feel better able to cope if you're replenishing your own strength at the same time, with exercise, plenty of relaxation and as much sleep as possible. If you've had a Caesarean delivery, you'll need to take life particularly easy, with extra rest and relaxation (see pages 110–11 for advice on exercise and breathing after a Caesarean birth).

After practicing the postnatal routine regularly, you can safely resume any form of exercise: try to include an activity like swimming, cycling or brisk walking that keeps your heart and lungs in good shape and builds up your stamina for the exacting job of parenthood.

————————————Stage one: the first week————————————

Two areas of the body need special attention in these first few days – the abdomen and the pelvic floor. You probably feel enthusiastic about starting abdominal exercises, and want to firm your sagging abdomen as soon as possible. However, you should start strengthening your pelvic floor before you progress on to the more advanced abdominal exercises in Stage two, as a weak and stretched pelvic floor can be weakened further by strong abdominal work. Try to exercise every day but don't go on for so long that you're exhausted: as in pregnancy, a little done often should be your goal.

You don't have to worry about your uterus, which will shrink back to its normal size within six weeks. During this process you may feel after pains, particularly after a second or subsequent baby. If you're breastfeeding, the pains may be especially noticeable when you're nursing. When they come, take a few deep breaths and try not to tense up against the pain – they don't last long. If you find them very troublesome, you may want to take painkillers.

BASIC ESSENTIALS
Incorporate these essentials into your daily
routine from the first day and keep them up
for three months – and beyond.

Breathing and abdominal tightening
Begin with slow breathing – it makes you feel
better and gently exercises your abdominal
muscles. Take a good breath in, lifting your
ribs up and out. Emphasize the out breath,
allowing your ribs to drop completely down
and in; at the same time, tighten your
abdomen. Do this gently at first and, as you

are able, increase the strength of the
movement, trying to pull your navel in
toward your spine. Don't breathe too deeply
or go on too long, as this may make you
dizzy, but do practice regularly.

As soon as you can, add a pelvic tilt (see
pages 14–15). Lie on your back, legs bent and
feet hip-width apart. As you breathe out, tilt
your pubic bone up, pulling your back into the
bed (below). Tighten your abdomen and
clench your buttocks at the same time. Try
this standing and sitting as well, and practice
it as often as you can remember it.

Pelvic floor
At first, there won't be much sensation or
control, but just try to find the pelvic floor
muscles again by doing quick tilts. Simply
squeeze and lift, gradually building up the
intensity, length and number of repetitions
over the next few weeks. If you have stitches,
remember that exercising your pelvic floor

helps them heal, by increasing the blood flow
to the area. Go on to the drawbridge exercise
on page 13 when you feel like it, as it's the
slow movement of this exercise that helps you
regain control and muscle tone. Aim to get
back to your normal routine of doing the
drawbridge as often as possible. To test your
progress after twelve weeks, see page 119.

Relaxation
left Lying face down, pillows raising your
hips, encourages all the pelvic organs to
return to their normal positions, as the
weight of your body presses gently down on
them. Don't read or prop yourself up on
your elbows in this position, as you'll over-
arch your back.

WHILE IN BED

Having a good stretch all over makes you feel better – do a pelvic tilt as you stretch.

It's important that you exercise your legs and feet while you're in bed, to prevent blood clots forming in the legs because of sluggish circulation. Exercise also discourages swelling in the legs – if you suffer from this, prop your feet up on some pillows while you rest.

Foot pedaling and circling

right Stretch your feet up and down, bending them up toward you and stretching them away, both feet working together or one foot coming up as the other goes down. You should also circle your feet as often as you can.

DURING THE FIRST WEEK

Aim to start practicing these exercises as well as the others on about the fourth day after delivery. Build up to six repetitions of each, but don't force yourself if you're still very tired and sore. If you find them difficult, just do what you can without too much strain.

Leg sliding and hip hitching

below Lie on your back, legs bent and feet hip-width apart. Do a pelvic tilt and slide one leg down a little, and back; keep your heel on the bed. Keep your back pressed into the support. Repeat with the other leg. As you do the exercise, put one hand under your back to check that you're holding the pelvic tilt – if your back rises, you're cheating. Better still, get a friend to check for you. If this is easy, progress to a pedaling motion, stretching alternate legs straight out while pressing your back into the support.

With one leg bent and the other straight, lengthen the straight leg by pushing the heel away from you, then shorten the same leg by pulling the heel toward you. Repeat several times with each leg.

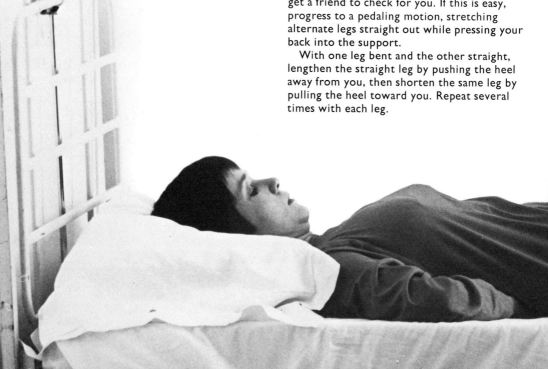

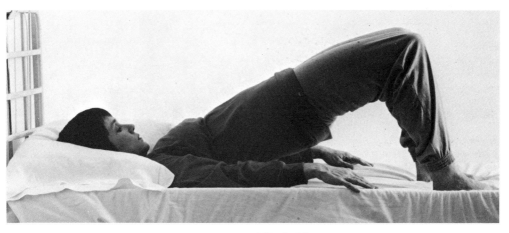

The bridge

above Lie on your back, legs bent and feet hip-width apart. Do a pelvic tilt and then push your hips up so your body forms a straight line from knees to shoulders. Squeeze and lift your pelvic floor at the same time and do the drawbridge exercise on page 13, as soon as you can.

Leg rolls

You can also start practicing the first stage of the leg-rolling exercise on page 114.

After a Caesarean birth

Immediately after the birth, you will have the usual postoperative problems of pain and fatigue. The incision will feel very sore at first and your abdomen will look big and out of shape. If you've had a general anesthetic, you may feel sick for the first day and if you had an emergency Caesarean birth, you may also be feeling shocked and bewildered. Whether the operation was planned or not, you need plenty of rest and time to recover, which can be difficult with all the demands of looking after your baby; but it's important to take time for relaxation as well as exercise, to help the healing process for your own sake and the baby's. It's also important to remember that this operation has a positive reward, in the shape of your baby. You may in fact feel better than you would have after a prolonged and difficult labor.

Getting out of bed

Nurses will help you out of bed and onto your feet as soon as possible after the birth to get your circulation going and to prevent blood clots developing in your legs. They'll encourage you to walk and if you try this, you'll be able to walk well within a few hours. Try to breathe deeply and straighten up as much as you can. Clasping both hands over the incision may help to give you confidence, and bracing your abdomen makes the movement less painful. If you need painkillers, don't be afraid to use them even if you're breastfeeding, as moving about is the top priority after the operation.

Breathing and exercise

You should be given expert advice and guidance on speeding your recovery after the operation, but you can also help yourself feel better with good breathing and gentle movement as you regain your strength. If a partner or friend can be there

Check for separation of the abdominal muscles

Before starting Stage two, check for separation of your abdominal muscles, as you did in pregnancy, following the instructions below. If the gap is more than two fingers wide, practice the exercise for realigning the muscles on page 47. Do it five times, and repeat several times throughout the day, aiming for 50 repetitions a day, which will take at most ten minutes. Repeat the test every week and as soon as the gap has lessened to two fingers' width or less, you can start on Stage two. If there's no improvement after six weeks, start on Stage two in any case, progressing slowly and carefully.

right Lie on your back, with your knees bent. Place the fingers of one hand below your navel. Gently press the fingers in and you'll probably feel a gap. Breathe in; as you breathe out, slowly lift your head and shoulders, tucking your chin in. You'll feel the muscle on either side of your fingers come together. How much? Is there hardly any gap at all, so your fingers come back to the surface? Can one finger stay in the gap, or more?

to encourage you, all the better: you need extra support to overcome the initial pain and any anxiety about hurting yourself. You may find it comforting to hold your abdomen with both hands when you begin to move and while you practice your breathing.

Start practicing the breathing and abdominal tightening on page 107 as soon as possible. The tightening stimulates the circulation in the abdominal area and so speeds healing; breathing well is particularly important after a general anesthetic, to clear out your lungs. The breathing exercise also helps to prevent pockets of wind forming in the intestines, which can be a painful problem during the first few days. If gas does collect in your intestines, you may feel it as referred pain in the armpits and shoulder area. If this happens, moving around helps to relieve the discomfort.

You should also practice "huffing" if you've had a general anesthetic. Breathe out forcefully, saying "ha", rather like a shallow cough. This helps to bring up any mucus that has collected in your lungs. If it's allowed to rest in your lungs, you may develop chest complications. Try to make two huffs on an out breath. If your chest is clear, you needn't bother to do any more. If it rattles, keep huffing at regular intervals until it stops. Sit upright as much as possible to help clear it – you can practice your breathing and exercises sitting up and it's also a good position for relaxation.

Even though you've not had a vaginal delivery, your pelvic floor still needs to be pulled up into place and made strong again after carrying the baby and after the operation, so practice the pelvic floor exercises on page 107, too. As soon as you are able, begin to add in the rest of the Stage one exercises: keeping your legs and feet moving is particularly important when you're in bed for longer than usual. Check with your medical adviser before starting on the stronger Stage two program on pages 112–17.

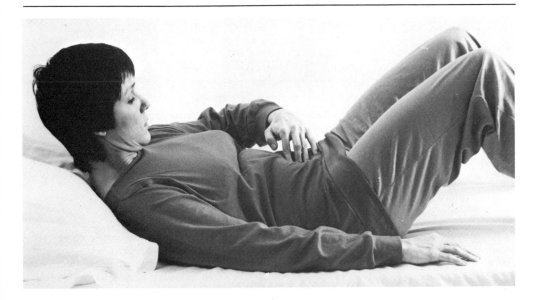

Stage two: weeks two to thirteen

Aim for six repetitions of each exercise throughout, except where stated otherwise. Begin by practicing curl downs, as often as you can until you feel confident. Once you're finding them easy, start on the basic routine; but if the new exercises are hard, or if you feel any pressure on your pelvic floor as you do them, go back to the curl downs for a few days. The basic routine consists of four exercises, and you do the progressive stages of each as you are able; the whole sequence shouldn't take you more than ten minutes. Remember to keep up your pelvic floor and pelvic tilt exercises as well. The curl ups may tire your neck, so roll it from side to side on the floor when you've finished them. You may like to use the exercises at the end if you have time for some extras or if you want some variation in your routine.

Preparation: curl downs
Sit with your legs bent, your feet hip-width apart and your arms folded, elbows lifted to shoulder level; you can hold your arms out in front at first if this is easier. Breathe in; as you breathe out, drop your chin, do a pelvic tilt (see pages 14–15), pulling in your abdomen. Lean back, until you feel your abdominal muscles tighten. Hold this position for a few seconds if possible, breathing normally – you can build up the holding time gradually, as you progress. Breathe in and sit upright.

BASIC ROUTINE
Curl ups
Lie on your back with your legs bent, feet hip-width apart, your hands on your thighs. Breathe in; as you breathe out, raise your head and shoulders, dropping your chin and reaching toward your knees.

Don't worry if your shoulders won't lift up at first – they will with practice. Gradually aim to lift yourself more slowly and to hold yourself up for longer periods. As this becomes easy, progress to:
- resting your hands on your chest
- clasping your hands behind your head.

Leg rolls
Lie on your back with your legs bent, knees together, hands on your ribs. Slowly lower your knees halfway to the floor, first to the right and then to the left, pressing your back into the floor as you pass through the central position. As this becomes easy, progress to:
- lowering your knees all the way to the floor on each side
- lowering your knees halfway to each side, legs bent up to your chest, arms outstretched
- lowering your knees to the floor, your legs bent up to your chest, arms outstretched, turning your head in the opposite direction.

Side bends
Lie on your back, legs straight and together, with your arms at your sides, palms flat on the sides of your thighs. Lift your head and bend to the right, sliding the right hand down your right leg; return to the center and bend to the left. Return to the center and rest. Repeat up to three times. As this becomes easy, progress to bending to each side twice, then three times, before lowering your head.

Diagonal curl ups
right Lie face up with your legs bent, feet hip-width apart, arms at your sides, palms up. Breathe in; as you breathe out, take your left hand over to touch the right. Breathe in as you return to the center. Repeat, taking your right hand to touch your left hand. As this becomes easy, progress to:
- taking your left hand to the outside of your right knee; repeat to the left
- taking both hands to the outside of your right knee; repeat to the left.

Postnatal exercise summary

STAGE ONE
Basic essentials
- breathing and abdominal tightening, with pelvic tilts
- pelvic floor exercises
- relaxation, lying face down

While in bed
- stretching
- foot pedaling and circling

End of the first week
- leg sliding

- hip hitching
- the bridge
- leg rolls, first part

STAGE TWO
Preparation
- curl downs

Basic routine
- curl ups
- leg rolls
- diagonal curl ups
- side bends

EXTRA EXERCISES

below Lie on one side, propped up on your elbow. Lift both feet up as high as you can and hold for a few moments. If you rest your free hand on your waist, you'll feel the muscles working. Repeat, lying on the other side. Work up to four repetitions.

left Kneel with your thighs hip-width apart, fold your arms and lift your elbows up to shoulder level. Sit to one side of your heels. Lift back up to the kneeling position. Then sit to the other side. Hold your arms outstretched at first if this is easier. Aim for six repetitions.

right You can do side bends kneeling, as well as lying. Kneel with your thighs hip-width apart, arms at your sides. Do a pelvic tilt (see pages 14–15) and make sure your posture is good. Bend to one side as far as you can, without leaning forward or back. Return to the center and bend the other way. Work up to six repetitions.

Kneel on all fours, your knees in line with your hips and your hands in line with your shoulders. Breathe in; and as you breathe out, bend one leg up, trying to touch the knee with your forehead. Breathe in and stretch the leg behind, keeping your head in line with your spine. Repeat with the other leg. Move one leg out sideways, resting your toes on the floor. Lift the leg slowly and hold it up for a few moments. Lower it slowly. Aim for six repeats and change legs.

Pelvic floor check
right After twelve weeks, try this test of your pelvic floor's strength. Jump up with your legs apart and cough at the same time. If there's no leak of urine, you know that you're in good shape. If you do leak, practice the drawbridge exercise on page 13 more often. If there's still no improvement after four months, consult your doctor.

Exercising with your baby

As your baby gets a little older and you become used to your postnatal exercise routine, you may want to introduce a little variety by exercising with her. Your baby will enjoy the movement and the attention and you'll have more fun if you have company. It also solves the problem of looking after her while you exercise. These are not the only exercises that you can do together – try adapting others from the postnatal routine.

Rest your baby on top of your abdomen to remind yourself to keep your back pressed into the floor for this exercise. Bend your legs and straighten them upward. Stretch them fully; spread them apart and bring them together a few times. Bend your legs for a rest. Restraighten them and lower one leg away from you a little and then the other, keeping your back pressed into the floor. Repeat a few times.

above Try curl ups (see page 113) with your baby resting on your shins.

below Sit with your legs straight out in front and "walk" forward and back on your hips.

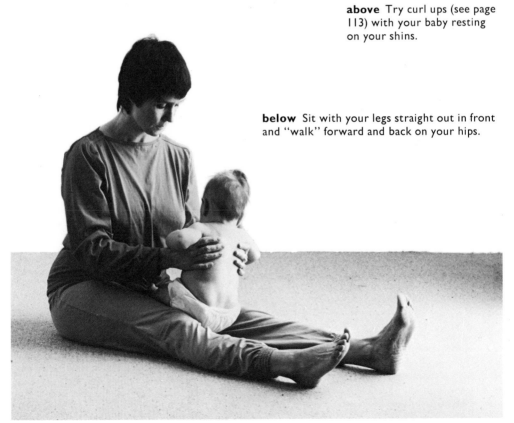

After your baby is born, you have to readjust your balance to the sudden loss of weight. Refer back to the section on pages 19–21 to remind yourself of the details of good posture. Help yourself to adjust by doing pelvic tilts regularly (see pages 14–15), tightening your abdomen and buttocks, and lifting your pelvic floor at the same time; try to become aware of the corset of muscle round your trunk, no matter how stretched it is at first. You'll be surprised at how quickly your abdomen begins to contract as you work at your postnatal routine and at re-adjusting your posture.

Avoid lifting heavy weights for six weeks after the birth if possible, but certainly for at least ten days. When you do start lifting, brace your pelvic floor and abdomen first and remember to bend your knees and keep your back straight (see pages 22–3). Make sure that your changing table is the right height for you – about the level of your navel. Tables are often too low; a chest of drawers may be an alternative; or, better and safer still, change the baby on the floor, where she can't fall (see page 124).

Feeding the baby
Feeding gives you the opportunity to enhance the relationship between you and your baby. Take time to enjoy it, cuddling your baby and watching her personality unfolding. This is also a good opportunity for you to relax, so a little preparation to make yourself comfortable is worth while. Whatever position you use for feeding, and whether you're bottle or breastfeeding, make sure that the arm holding the baby is well supported. If you're breastfeeding, use pillows or cushions to raise your baby to the right level for sucking, so you don't have to bend or twist, and keep your body as symmetrical as you can.

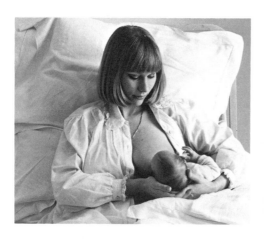

If you've had a Caesarean delivery, try resting the baby on some pillows beside you instead of on your sore abdomen; it's comfortable if you've had a normal delivery, too. This is also a good position to use for feeding twins.

If you find sitting up uncomfortable, because of painful stitches, or if you've had a Caesarean birth, try lying on your side with the baby alongside you. This is also good for night feedings, as you can rest as you feed.

below Once you are used to it, sitting cross-legged on the floor is a perfect position for feeding or playing with your baby, as your lap with a cushion in it makes a lovely cradle. If you feel more comfortable, lean against a wall, supporting yourself with cushions.

above If you like to sit on a chair, choose one that allows your feet to rest comfortably on the floor, and sit well back in it. Raise one leg by resting your foot on a stool or a pile of books and use a cushion to bring the baby up to the right level to feed. Change legs when you move your baby to the other side.

Carrying the baby
right With a baby carrier, adjust your posture to the extra weight just as you did when you were pregnant, centering your pelvis, lifting your ribs and dropping your shoulders.

far right Babies usually enjoy lying face down, and carrying them on one arm allows you to remain well balanced – but change arms from time to time.

Posture and key positions

Use the key positions (see pages 25–41) as often as possible so that your back remains strong and supple, and your hips and legs keep their mobility. You'll find that you can easily incorporate them into your everyday routine of looking after the baby. Below are some examples, but if you improvise you'll find many more ways of adapting the positions.

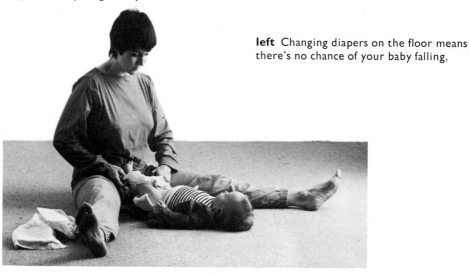

left Changing diapers on the floor means there's no chance of your baby falling.

right If you're feeding your baby solids, squatting brings you down to her level and ensures that you don't strain your back.

left Babies love to be gently massaged and rubbed – if you use your legs as support, both your hands are free.

For every couple, the postnatal period is filled with excitement and new sensations; but life is seen through a haze of fatigue. The baby makes constant demands – erratic feeding and unpredictable sleeping patterns make it hard to eat properly, let alone make love! Add to this the massive hormonal adjustments and physical healing taking place in the mother's body and it's hardly surprising that sex becomes a conscious issue rather than a spontaneous expression of love. Understanding the physical changes taking place makes it easier to cope. Your uterus has to shrink back to its normal size, the extra fluid in your body has to be lost and any cuts or tears in the perineum or abdomen have to heal. Breastfeeding has to be established, or suppressed: if you're bottle feeding, it will take four to six weeks for your ovaries to revert to their usual function but if you're breastfeeding this can be delayed. Either way it's essential that you use some form of contraception, as you can't be sure when you will first ovulate, but the method that you choose depends on various factors, such as whether you've had stitches and whether you're breastfeeding, so consult your doctor or clinic. If you've been using a diaphragm, remember that you may need a different size.

When you resume intercourse depends on the state of your perineum and your state of mind. If you've had stitches, you'll probably want to wait until you can see and feel that they're completely healed. Make sure you go to your doctor with any problems; you can't enjoy sex if you're in pain. Try doing pelvic floor exercises (see page 107) as soon as you can to help you heal and also reactivate your sexual responses. You may find that even after the stitches have healed you have fears of penetration; make sure your partner knows your worries – you probably need a little more time and extra tenderness and reassurance.

During the first few weeks of breastfeeding, you may find you're less interested in sex: hormonal changes and lactation slow down your responses and babies always seem to cry at just the wrong moment. However, intense sexual feelings are common at this time, in the broader sense of longing to be lovingly held, cuddled and stroked. You may want this closeness to develop into sex, but for many couples this is a time to be patient, loving and caring while trying not to make extra demands. You may find that mutual pleasuring and oral sex are initially the most satisfying ways to enjoy each other.

The passionate involvement many women feel with a new baby is very satisfying; but gradually the mother turns back toward her partner again, often with more powerful sexual feelings than before, sometimes when breastfeeding has settled down, sometimes not until after weaning. When you decide to try vaginal penetration, remember that your natural secretions may be diminished for some weeks, even if you've had a Caesarean birth, so you should use a lubricating jelly in and around the entrance of the vagina. If the woman lies on top, she can control the depth of penetration and she also avoids pressure on her breasts, which may be tender and full of milk. The first time you make love will probably not be wonderful. Be patient and remember it's only a matter of time before you're back to normal and probably better than before the birth. Enjoying and giving pleasure in love-making becomes an extension of the total experience of childbirth – more than ever you can appreciate your body and respond to your own feelings and those of your partner with passion and abandon.

Exercise and posture

Barlow, Wilfred, *The Alexander Technique*, Knopf, 1973.

Bertherat, Thérèse, and Bernstein, Carol, *The Body Has Its Reasons*, Pantheon, 1977.

Bing, Elisabeth, *Moving Through Pregnancy*, Bantam, 1976.

Leboyer, Frederick, *Inner Beauty, Inner Light: Yoga for Pregnant Women*, Knopf, 1978.

Mitchell, Laura, and Dale, Barbara, *Simple Movement*, John Murray, London, 1980.

Noble, Elizabeth, *Essential Exercises for the Childbearing Year* (2nd ed., rev.), Houghton Mifflin, 1982.

Relaxation

Krishnamurti, Jiddu, *Meditations*, Harper & Row, 1979.

Madders, Jane, *Stress and Relaxation*, Arco, 1979.

Mitchell, Laura, *Simple Relaxation*, Atheneum, 1979.

Pre- and postnatal sex

Bing, Elisabeth, and Colman, Libby, *Making Love During Pregnancy*, Bantam, 1977.

Fromm, Erich, *The Art of Loving*, Harper & Row, 1974.

Massage

Downing, George, *The Massage Book*, Random House/Bookworks, 1972.

Leboyer, Frederick, *Loving Hands*, Knopf, 1976.

Montagu, Ashley, *Touching: The Human Significance of the Skin*, Columbia University Press, 1971.

Caring for yourself

Boston Women's Health Book Collective, *Our Bodies, Ourselves*, Simon & Schuster, 1976.

Brewer, Gail (ed.), *The Pregnancy-After-30 Workbook*, Rodale, 1978.

Brewer, Gail and Tom, *What Every Pregnant Woman Should Know*, Random House, 1977.

Lappé, Frances, *Diet for a Small Planet*, Ballantine Books, 1971.

Noble, Elizabeth, *Having Twins*, Houghton Mifflin, 1980.

Labor

Bradley, Robert, *Husband-Coached Childbirth*, Harper & Row, 1965.

Dick-Reed, Grantly, *Childbirth Without Fear*, Harper & Row, 1972.

Kitzinger, Sheila, *Birth at Home*, Oxford University Press, 1979.

Kitzinger, Sheila, *Education and Counselling for Childbirth*, Schocken, 1979.

Kitzinger, Sheila, *The Experience of Childbirth*, Taplinger, 1972.

Leboyer, Frederick, *Birth Without Violence*, Knopf, 1975.

Macfarlane, Aidan, *The Psychology of Childbirth*, Harvard University Press, 1977.

Nilsson, Lennart, *A Child Is Born*, Delacorte Press, 1967.

Breastfeeding and becoming a family

Ewy, Rodger and Donna, *Preparation for Breastfeeding*, Doubleday, 1975.

Flanagan, Geraldine, *The First Nine Months of Life*, Simon & Schuster, 1962.

Kitzinger, Sheila, *The Experience of Breast Feeding*, Penguin, 1980.

Leach, Penelope, *Your Baby and Child*, Knopf, 1978.

Levy, Janine, *The Baby Exercise Book*, Pantheon, 1975.

Messenger, Máire, *The Breastfeeding Book*, Van Nostrand Reinhold, 1982.

Stern, Daniel, *The First Relationship: Infant and Mother*, Harvard University Press, 1977.

Winnicott, D. W., *The Child, the Family and the Outside World*, Penguin, 1969.

Useful addresses

American Academy of Husband-Coached Childbirth, Box 5224, Sherman Oaks, CA 91413. (213) 788-6662.

American College of Nurse Midwives, 1522 K St. N.W., Suite 1120, Washington, D.C. 20005. (202) 347-5447.

American Public Health Association, Maternal-Child Health Section, 1015 15th St. N.W., Washington, D.C. 20005. (202) 789-5600.

American Society for Psychoprophylaxis in Obstetrics (ASPO/Lamaze), 1411 K St. N.W., Washington, D.C. 20005. (202) 783-7050.

Cooperative Childbirth Network, 14 Truesdale Drive, Croton-on-Hudson, NY 10520. (914) 271-6474.

International Childbirth Education Association (ICEA), 5636 W. Burleigh St., Milwaukee, WI 53210. (414) 445-7470.

National Association for Parents and Professionals for Safe Alternatives in Childbirth (NAPSAC), P.O. Box 267, Marble Hill, MO 63764. (314) 238-2010.

The National Midwives Association, P.O. Box 163, Princeton, NJ 08540. (609) 799-1942.